THE WRITING OF HISTORY

THE
WRITING OF HISTORY

Adrien Antoine

BY

JEAN JULES JUSSERAND
FORMER AMBASSADOR FROM FRANCE
LATE PRESIDENT OF THE AMERICAN HISTORICAL ASSOCIATION

WILBUR CORTEZ ABBOTT
PROFESSOR OF HISTORY AT HARVARD UNIVERSITY

CHARLES W. COLBY

AND

JOHN SPENCER BASSETT
PROFESSOR OF HISTORY AT SMITH COLLEGE
SECRETARY OF THE AMERICAN HISTORICAL ASSOCIATION

43504

CHARLES SCRIBNER'S SONS

NEW YORK   CHICAGO   BOSTON

ATLANTA   SAN FRANCISCO

D
13
J8

PREFACE

The committee of the American Historical Association on the Writing of History was appointed in 1920, and consisted of His Excellency Jean Jules Jusserand, ambassador from France, chairman, with Doctor Charles William Colby and Professor Wilbur Cortez Abbott the other members. In 1922 Professor John Spenser Bassett, secretary of the association, was added to the committee.

Back of the creation of the committee was a realization by the Executive Council of the association that the writing of history in the United States was not in a satisfactory state. The Council desired the committee to make a study of the matter as it exists at present and to present a report in which appears such a frank and helpful analysis as they think the situation demands. The Council took notice of the general protest of a large portion of the public against the heaviness of style characteristic of much of the history now being written. They thought it necessary to do something to awaken young students and his-

torians to a realization of the part good expression must play in enabling history to maintain a place in the world of letters. To them it
did not seem advisable to accept the existing
situation as the best to be expected, nor to
relinquish without a struggle the hope that
historical information may be presented in
such a manner as to make the reading of it
pleasant if not delightful.

In laying out the work assigned to them the
members of the committee concluded to treat
the subject in three large phases. First in development and in nature seemed to lie an examination of the existing situation, with some
discussion of how it came about. Let the examination be made frankly, without undue
attack and undue criticism. Let us see in what
respect history has gained and in what respect
it has lost in the esteem of the public during
the last half century. If we can agree upon
this general phase of the problem, we shall lay
the foundation of an intelligent consideration
of the other phases.

About one fact in this connection we can
hardly have two opinions: Fifty years ago historians like Bancroft and Prescott stood side
by side with the great poets at the top of the

world of letters. From the men of their day they received esteem, public honors, and wealth. They lived like proconsuls over provinces of literary expression. To-day the historian's influence has waned. He is no longer to be compared with the lordly proconsul, but rather to the hard-working centurion, whose labors held together the military units on which rested the Roman authority in the province. He is, perhaps, a more genuine writer of truth and more industrious; but he is not at the top of the world as formerly. In this report an effort is made to burrow through this fact, so that the young historian may comprehend it and establish his own reflections upon it.

Another general phase of the problem before us was the consideration of style of expression in historical writing. The craftsmanship of the historian is a subject of great importance and not often enough considered. Perhaps it is necessary for some minds to have settled the question of the possibility of having good style in good histories. Can writers devoted to research and filled with the scientific spirit be true to their purposes, and at the same time write history that has the charm of literature? And if that can be done, what suggestions can be made of a practical nature for helping the young historian to write in such a manner? The members of the committee think that here is a profitable field of discussion, in which wisdom may be gained if certitude may not be reached.

Still another phase of the problem which seems to demand consideration is the training of historians in expression. It involves an examination of the rôle that is being played, or may be played, by the history departments in our universities, where historical students are prepared for their careers. While it is true that we have had some good historians who are self-trained, it is probable that the large majority of our historians of the future will come out of our graduate schools of history. It is here that are formed standards of taste and method. Here must begin any improvement that is to be made in history writing in this country. The thoughts presented on this phase of the general subject are given as a means of calling the attention of teachers and students to the responsibility that lies on the graduate school. It is believed that neither, and least of all the students, will be willing, once they consider the matter, to ignore the necessity of working in the most conscientious manner for clear and orderly historical expression. Without such expression they fail in their efforts to make themselves into good historians.

These three parts of the report, it was felt, needed something to bind them together, and the chairman of the committee was urged to write such a summation. He willingly agreed, and the result is the first part of the report, serving as a bond, uniting the other parts and serving as a call to duty. In his long and honored career in this country as ambassador of the French Republic, M. Jusserand has been vitally interested in the progress of history here, as in the progress of every other branch of intellectual life, and he has taken notable parts in promoting it. He has written about our history, he has encouraged others to write about it, and he has served as president of the American Historical Association. His part of this report is his parting gift to his American colleagues in the field of historical endeavor. By the common consent of the other members of the committee, the paper of M. Jusserand has been arranged first in the order of publication, not only because of its excellence but because of their high respect for his position in the historian's profession.

Each member of the committee, after writing his own part of the report, has submitted it to the other members; and he has accepted or rejected, as he saw fit, the criticisms he has received, with the understanding that he assumes responsibility for his own part alone. The committee, therefore, presents to the reader a series of chapters containing opinions based on the views of the individual writer, united only in a common desire to promote a serious effort to improve historical writing and to see that history maintains its place as a form of literature.

The reader will observe a small amount of repetition in the four parts of the report. The subject is so essentially united that it seemed impossible to avoid such repetitions without interfering with the freedom of treatment which was accepted in the beginning. It is believed that the reader will be pleased that each writer has given full range to his ideas and that the presentation of some ideas by more than one person will add pleasure to the reading because it gives variety of expressing similar ideas and sometimes divergent interpretations of the same thing.

Although it is assumed that the reader will not doubt this assurance with respect of the repetitions in this book, it was decided to give him the benefit of all the facts and to arrange the last three parts of the report in the book in the order in which they were finished and handed to the secretary of the committee. They were all written independently and without any restrictions on the individuals writing them.

It should be clearly understood that this report is not to be taken as expressing the official opinion of the American Historical Association, or of a majority of its members. No one statement could embody precisely the composite view of so large an organization on any but a most general matter. The significance of the effort is this: The Council representing the association felt that something should be done to improve history writing, and that the thing most likely to do good in that field was to have four of its members study the subject and submit the results for the consideration of all who are interested. Other persons than this committee might have come to different conclusions. In any case their report would be, like this, an expression of the ideas of those who made it. It is not intended to be dogmatic. If it stimulates the student to examine the subject for himself and to resolve that he will endeavor in the most conscientious manner to write the best history that in him lies, it will do all that can be desired; for it is vain to ask that all men write alike, and the best writer of history is he who lets swing the arm God gave him, always remembering his duty to be truthful and to reverence the things that are honorable.

J. S. B.

CONTENTS

THE HISTORIAN'S WORK

JEAN JULES JUSSERAND

LATE PRESIDENT OF THE AMERICAN HISTORICAL ASSOCIATION

THE HISTORIAN'S WORK

HOW history should be written has been the subject of ardent discussions ever since history has been written. The complaint that the method is not what it should be is a millennial one; it was loud in Greek and Roman times and has been renewed since, sometimes with acerbity, in most of the civilized nations.

The chief reason is not that the problem is so difficult, but that, as history deals with individuals, families, and nations, it excites passions, and passions do not facilitate the solution of problems.

But for passion, the question would appear simple enough to open-minded people. To remember what is history is indeed to solve the problem.

History is not simply an art, nor simply a science; as the accompanying papers well show, it participates in the nature of both. In the hunt for facts and the ascertaining of truth, the historian must be as conscientious

as the scientist. In the presentation he must be
an artist, a true one, not one of those who favor
vain embellishments and are not, therefore,
true artists (*vilia miretur vulgus*), but of those
who bring you as near as possible to the realities, showing them as they are, in their glory
or their misery, simply putting between the
reader and the facts a transparent, crystal-like
glass, not a colored one.

Art is selection. Historians must select; they
can not write history life-size; among thousands of facts they have to choose those especially important or especially characteristic.
"An inconspicuous action," says Plutarch, "a
word, a joke, will ofttimes better reveal a character than the bloodiest fights or the most important battles and sieges." A heavy responsibility rests with historians; they must have
prepared themselves by thought, method,
study, observation, and hard work, to judge
well.

And this responsibility is now all their own.
They have no longer the excuse of censorship.
They have not to apprehend the interference
of a James I, reproving a Raleigh for his too
severe judgments on Spain, or of a Napoleon
rebuking even long-dead Tacitus for having

[4]

been too hard on emperors. They can freely speak their minds; they are all-powerful. But this boon carries with it terrible dangers. Limitless power is begotten of tyrants. Only well-tempered souls can resist the lure: the whole course of history is an evidence thereof. Has it never happened even in our days that some newspapers acted as tyrants, all-powerful, unchecked, practically irresponsible?

The honest man, the honest historian, will check himself and be his own censor, or, in other words, will take for his censors and guiding lights Learning, Truth, Justice.

The historian's means of communication with the public is writing, as color is for painters. An historian who uses so dull a style that he will not be read is as useless as a painter who should use invisible colors. He is, moreover, sure not to do justice to realities, thus swerving from truth, for realities are not dull. Those for whom they are so suffer from a dull mind and a dull heart. In them is the fault, not in the things.

All this has been said thousands of years ago, and would have been said then once for all if those same passions, if waywardness, if personal interest had not periodically clouded the issue, so that the same axioms have had to be periodically enunciated again.

A century and a half before Christ, Polybius was writing: "Truth is for history what eyes are for animals. Remove the eyes of animals, they become useless; remove truth from history, it is no longer of any use. Whether friends or foes be in question, we must only follow justice. . . . What must serve as a foundation for the historian's judgment is not the men who did the deeds, but the deeds themselves. . . . The historian must not try to move his readers by tales of wonder, nor imagine what may have been said. . . . This he must leave to tragic poets and limit himself to what has been really said or done."

Eighteen centuries ago Lucian of Samosata assigned to himself just the same task that the American Historical Association has assigned to us, the members of its committee, and he tried to point out "the way history should be written." His chief conclusions might be adopted by our committee. The historian, according to him, must be above all truthful, impartial, fearless. "His only duty is to relate what has happened; he will be unable to say it if he is afraid of Artaxerxes, whose physician he is. . . . Incorruptible, independent, a friend of truth and sincerity, he must, as the comic poet says, call a fig a fig, and a bark a bark, allowing nothing to hatred nor to love, sparing nobody out of friendship, shame, or respect, an impartial judge prejudiced against no one, granting to all their due." A history without truth is a history without use. A poet "can tie winged horses to a chariot; he can cause chariots to fly over the waters"; an historian can not. "Praise and blame must be moderate, bestowed with circumspection, free from calumny and flattery."

His style will be "steady and quiet, perfectly luminous. . . . The chief, the only, aim of style is to put facts in a clear light, with no concealment, no obsolete words nor words having a smack of the tavern or the public square. His terms must be, at the same time, intelligible to the vulgar and approved by the experts. . . . Brevity is always commendable, but especially when you have much to say." A style that delights will not be blamed; on the contrary, "it has its usefulness, as beauty enhances the merit of an athlete"; but the athlete and history can at need do without it.

This tuition was often resumed in the course

of ages by men who, in order to give it, did not need to remember any predecessors, but only to consider what history is. The rules for writing history, said Cicero, in a well-known passage of his *De Oratore*, "are obvious. Who does not perceive that its chief law is never to dare say anything false, and never dare withhold anything true? The slightest suspicion of hatred or favor must be avoided. That such should be the foundations is known to all; the materials with which the building will be raised consist of facts and words."

The same in the modern world. Long before Ranke rendered his memorable services to history, the well-known author of the *De Republica*, Jean Bodin, wrote on the threshold of his *Methodus ad facilem Historiarum Cognitionem:* "History, that is to say a truthful narrative" ("*Historia, id est vera narratio*"), 1566.

Truth thus being the rule, facts being the material out of which the building will be raised by that combination of artist and scientist which the true historian, the true architect, should be—facts must be sought for, sifted, tested, so that imitation marble be not accepted instead of marble, nor painted plaster instead of stone. Hence that immense effort,

till then unparalleled, due chiefly to the
French Benedictines of the seventeenth and
eighteenth centuries, to do an honest mason's
work and place reliable material at the disposal
of the architect, of the historian. "I attempt a
new kind of antiquarian research," wrote Ma-
billon at the beginning of his *De Re Diploma-
tica*, 1681. "It concerns those old documents
which, by common agreement, are the historian's chief guide, provided they be genuine."
He will show how this material should be assayed.

Montfaucon, another Benedictine, is careful
always to quote his sources: "I have composed
this history (*Les Monumens de la Monarchie
Françoise*, 1729) on the originals themselves,
ever quoting in the margin of my Latin text
the authors and chronologists whom I have
used, often giving their very words, especially
when they are not clear and may be interpreted
in different ways." The reader will decide. He
has always gone to the earliest sources, never
"adorning his narrative at the expense of
truth."

Bouquet begins in 1738 the publication of
his immense *Recueil des historiens des Gaules
et de la France*. "Each volume," he announces

in his introduction, "will include a preface and critical notes and tables. Dates will be inscribed on the margin when not given in the text and will be rectified when there is need."

"Without a trustworthy chronology," says François Clément, also a Benedictine, the author of the huge *Art de vérifier les Dates,* "history would be but a darksome chaos"; he will come to the help of all those who, interested in history, "study it in its sources, read charters, original deeds, and try to interpret medals and inscriptions."

The like had never been seen. "No page in the annals of learning," says Gooch, "is more glorious than that which records the labors of these humble but mighty scholars." * The example was followed; historians were staggered. "The universal progress of science during the two last centuries, the art of printing, and other obvious causes have filled Europe with such a multitude of histories and with such vast collections of historical material, that the term of human life is too short for the study or even the perusal of them." So wrote William Robertson, 1769, in the preface of a history, not of

* *History and Historians in the Nineteenth Century* (1913), **p. 4.**

the world nor of a nation, but of a man, Emperor Charles V.

What would he say to-day? For the impetus has not slackened; far from it; research has become more and more exact, and its field, which now includes economic and social problems, art, manners, scientific and all other kinds of progress, moral improvements or retrogressions, has ceaselessly increased, all nations vying with each other, Germany playing in her turn a conspicuous part in the work, England printing or calendaring the vast treasure of her records, and America showing, especially of late years, praiseworthy zeal and efficiency.

The materials are thus within the reach of all, abundant, assayed, reliable. History is, however, less popular in America, we are told, less read, less enjoyed than in times gone by. In the flux and reflux of human tastes and dispositions, this is probably but a temporary phase; and it will be shortened if would-be historians and those who teach them remember the above-mentioned fundamental principles of the genre.

They are, as we have seen, simple enough. To the utmost that is humanly possible, history must conform to truth, and this is made comparatively easy by the new methods more and more abundantly and skilfully taught in the universities, and by the accumulated wealth of accessible documents; it must, at the same time, be as interesting as life itself, which again is comparatively easy for any one who knows how to look at life. Men and nations toil, labor, try, fail, suffer, succeed, love, hate, discover, stumble, die. It seems scarcely credible that it be possible to present a true picture of such events and not be interesting.

Students there be who have failed in this out of fear, overawed by the stately pronouncement of some that if history is interesting it can not be scientific, and if it is scientific it can not be interesting. For safety they have made a display of their science, pleased a few critics, and frightened away the public. There is, of course, no truth in such a dictum; the more scientific, the fuller of life history should be, since it would present a more direct picture of life. The proofs, the references, the discussions of most points should be put at their proper place; that is, in the notes and appendices. The cook has to peel his potatoes, but he does not peel them on the dining-room table.

The men presented to the reader have been

alive in their day; they must, if our knowledge of the period allows, be presented to him as they were when alive, not mere *simulacra*, empty names. "I do not know a man," said Fénelon, "by knowing only his name." The same with nations, pictures of which reduced to wars and princely deeds have long ceased to suffice. "After having read two or three thousand descriptions of battles and the text of some hundreds of treaties, I found," said Voltaire, "that I was scarcely better informed than before."

In a lecture on "Picturesqueness in History" (*Cornhill Magazine*, March, 1897), the historian of the papacy, Bishop Creighton (who rightly notes that it is "not absolutely necessary to be dull in order to prove that you can write"), seems to imply that picturesqueness is the attribute of great men and great events, so that the writer prone to avail himself of this element of interest and success runs the risk of "passing hastily from one strongly marked personality to another, from one striking event to another." But such a writer should not write at all, since he does not know how to see. The simplest lives may chance to be as picturesque as any. What simpler, yet what

more picturesque than the life of the Vicar of
Wakefield! Many people have elbowed him
without suspecting it, because they do not
know how to see. But a Goldsmith sees it and
makes us see it.

The situation is somewhat different in
France; more heated, one might almost say
more rabid, than ever before, discussions rent,
some years ago, the quiet halls of Clio, and the
problem of how history should be taught and
written, over which our minds were ever busy
(Daunou's *Cours d'études historiques* is in
twenty volumes),* was the subject of contests
as passionate as if the question had been of a
social reform or a change in the constitution.
The very bitterness of the dispute was a proof
of the prime importance attached to the historical art. History is, in fact, abundantly read
in France, no work of this sort with any merit
in it fails to find readers; reviews meant, not
for specialists, but for the general public, like
the *Revue des Deux Mondes*, the *Revue de Paris*,
the *Correspondant*, the *Revue de France*, etc.,
accept with alacrity articles on historical subjects. Each volume of the *Histoire de la Nation*

---

* Posthumously published, 1842. The lectures had been delivered
at the Collège de France 1819 *et seq.*

Française published under the editorship of **M.**
Hanotaux, and which will be in fifteen volumes, has twenty thousand purchasers secure
on the day it is issued. Over twenty thousand copies have been sold of the monumental *Histoire de France* of Lavisse, in twenty-
eight volumes, the last of which appeared in
1922.

For the adoption of a proper style in historical works, clear as plate-glass, the French student is prepared by his national love of clarity
and logic, by the nature and complexion of his
own native language, and by the tuition he re-
ceives. This tuition is, so to say, of every in-
stant and begins almost from childhood. The
use by children of an inappropriate word is
oftener than not checked at the family board;
much more at college, where, moreover, the
study of the classics, the themes and versions,
the reading of the best authors, discipline the
young minds, oblige them to ascertain the real
value of an expression, to discard redundant
words, to avoid the vain flourish of useless epi-
thets and adverbs. Visiting England in 1710,
G. L. Lesage, a Protestant refugee, noted with
surprise that, "Rarely does the conversation
turn there upon the appropriateness of a word

or upon the correctness of a way of speaking."
Not so in France.

The class recently created in colleges and
called "Rhétorique supérieure," or "Première
supérieure," is rendering in this respect immense service; nothing "rhetorical," however, in the teaching; pupils are, on the contrary, shown how to chasten their language.*

This is being taught with rejuvenated vigor
but there is nothing new in it. Such precepts,
those of common sense, have been enunciated
throughout the ages, especially as concerns history, by men like Cicero two thousand, and
by Fénelon and by "le bon Rollin" two hundred years ago. Said Cicero: "The tone must
be simple and easy, the style firm in its even-
ness, without the asperity of judicial discussions and with none of the shafts used in plead-
ings before a court." Said Rollin: "A clever
teacher will point out to his pupils the graces
and beauties to be found in an historian; but
he will not suffer his pupils to be dazzled by a
vain fulguration of words, to prefer flowers to
fruits, to be less attentive to truth itself than
to its ornaments, nor to make more of an his-

* The weekly programme consists of four hours of French, four of
Latin, four of Greek, four of history, four of philosophy, four of
English or German.

torian's eloquence than of his exactness and his faithful rendering of facts."

Tuition is necessary. To trust to chance, to casual reading, to inborn gifts is to run great risks. In his *Writing of English* Mr. P. J. Hartog, registrar of the University of London, takes for his theme the propositions that "the English boy can not write English, not being taught to write English; the French boy can write French because he is taught how to write." Maybe, wanting a reform, he exaggerates. He is, however, corroborated by Mr. J. H. Fowler in his *Teaching of English Composition*.

All this applies to the American 'prentice historian, as to all others, more perhaps to him than to some others, because he does not grow up so habitually as in France, for instance, in a *milieu* where such traditional disciplines of the mind are practised. He may be tempted, for that very reason, to scorn them as old-fashioned theories; but he had better be careful, since they are not the vain inventions of rhetoricians or the legacy of an "effete" Old World, but the outcome of common sense. It is old-fashioned, certainly, to say that two and two make four, but no amount of deriding will cause it to make five.

He must especially be careful never to apply, as happens, big words to little occasions: for when great occasions come, what will he say? "The wordes," said Chaucer, "mote be cosin to the dede."

There is the overbold beginner and the over-timorous one. The first, unhampered by knowledge, launches into immature generalizations; he has vast views; ignoring pitfalls, he scorns his elders and their conscientious care, which he calls timidity. He does not suspect that he may thus cramp his own career, burdening himself with hasty propositions which he will drag rattling behind him his life long. Much better develop logically: first learn the trade, then practise it; learn how to search for truth in the maze of documents, and to use the appropriate style.

The beginner's first attempt will usually be his dissertation or thesis for a doctor's degree; conscientious research should be the chief merit, conclusions and generalizations should not be excluded, but must be guarded, because the author's acquaintance with men and events, past and present, is necessarily limited. No useful generalization or synthesis is possible without much knowledge and psychology.

The access to documents has been greatly facilitated in America as elsewhere. But there are documents and documents; a penetrating spirit, a good deal of wisdom, an ever-present care, are necessary in order not to be imposed upon. There are honest documents and dishonest ones; they all say: "Listen, trust me, I was there"; but some were and some were not. All of them should be as severely cross-examined as witnesses in a court of law.

Much has been printed; not all, far from it. Lord Acton has recalled that when the Vatican archives were sent to France, they filled 3,239 cases, "and they are not the richest." The beginner, who must try, in his dissertation, to bring some new fact to light, will have to study unprinted material; it affords him his best chance for treasure trove. If he succeeds, as he will with persistence and "flair," he must, however, be careful to avoid the fault of some who thereupon heed only the unprinted and scorn the rest, resembling those tourists who have no cease until they have got access to some private gallery, but merely glance at the public ones, where the best pictures may happen to be.

The historian, who is not a mere collector of

documents, has to express views, to summar-
ize, to conclude. This was, in former days, his
hour of delight; a romantic in romantic times,
unmindful of any Lucian, he flew, like Shake-
speare's poet, "an eagle flight, bold and forth
on," thinking that his pen could rival a poet's,
and give

> "to airy nothing
> A local habitation and a name."

This is nowadays for the historian his hour
of anguish, the moment when the timid beginner will run away; what will critics say if he
dares raise his eyes from his texts? But if he
has conscientiously studied his facts, his documents, gone to all the accessible sources of information, well weighed his evidence, he should
have no qualms; he has done his duty. And
that duty includes the admission into his work
of a certain amount of possibilities and prob-
abilities. He is exhuming the past; his task re-
sembles that of the paleontologist who does not
always find complete skeletons and must risk
a hypothesis as to what the missing parts were
like; to do so successfully as proved by later
discoveries was the glory of Cuvier. When they
publish sketches of their finds, paleontologists
show by a plain line what the earth has yielded,

and by a dotted one what, according to their speculations, the rest would have been like. The historian must do the same, that the reader may know what is certain and what is only probable. His verifyings will be especially severe when he has to deal with a particularly picturesque fact or man. Picturesque events or people abound in history and are as real as the most vulgar, but they have always, for obvious reasons, caught the fancy of the falsifier, who has embellished or invented many; hence the need of extra care. But to discard a fact simply because picturesque is as unscientific as to admit it without proof. Truth, it must be acknowledged, is rarely as clearly defined as a black line on a sheet of white paper drawn by a firm hand. Men would be too happy; there is a sort of haze about it. Many adopt as the proper level the upper limit of the haze, especially when an attractive, momentous, picturesque event is in question. Wiser people will choose the lower. Of the first, the reader will soon grow diffident; he will feel safe with the second and trust them.

Another delicate question is whether the historian must be so perfectly objective that no trace of his nationality should appear in his writings. Many among the best historians and critics agree that none should. He must be, said Lucian, "a stranger in his own writings, without a country, without laws, without a prince, indifferent to what this one or that one may say, only relating what has happened." He must give to his compatriots their due, not more; to his country's enemies their due, not less. He must not imitate that writer who compares our general to Achilles and the King of the Persians to Thersites. He apparently forgets that Achilles is more illustrious by his victory over Hector than if he had killed Thersites."

In his *Lettre à l'Académie Française*, to whom he recommends the devising of a treatise on the writing of history (which, however, that august body never devised), Fénelon is no less positive: "The good historian belongs to no time or country; though he loves his own he never flatters it in any respect. The French historian must remain neutral between France and England; he must as willingly praise Talbot as Du Guesclin; he renders the same justice to the military talents of the Prince of Wales (the Black Prince) as to the wisdom of Charles V."

Speaking at the Collège de France, on the 8th of December, 1870, in the capital besieged then by the Germans, Gaston Paris said: "I stand absolutely and without reserve for this doctrine, that science has no other object than truth, and truth for itself, with no heed as to the consequences good or bad, regrettable or fortunate, which that truth may entail. He who, from a patriotic, religious, or even moral motive permits himself, in the facts he studies, in the conclusions he draws, the least dissimulation, the slightest alteration, is unworthy of a place in that great laboratory where probity is a title for admission more indispensable than cleverness."

Describing the attitude of mind in which he wrote his *Origines de la France Contemporaine,* Taine declared that he had studied the events as impartially as if the question had been of the revolutions in Florence or Athens. He said also: "An historian may be permitted to act like a naturalist; I looked at my subject as if I had been looking at the metamorphosis of an insect."

His sincerity is undoubted. Can one say that he succeeded? Can one say that it is possible to succeed to the extent which was his ideal?

The most ardent propagators of this doctrine, the Germans, when they came to the practice of it, certainly failed. Even the beautiful motto selected for the *Monumenta Germaniae*, though a mere collection of texts, does not forecast absolute impartiality: *Sanctus amor patriae dat animum*. "Read the German historians of the last half century," wrote Fustel de Coulanges; "you will be struck by the extent to which their historical theories perfectly agree with their patriotism."

But when due limits have been observed, one ought not to be too severe on the historian unable to veil entirely his nationality or his faith, especially if, as is the case with men like Albert Sorel or La Gorce, he confesses that such indeed is the case, which is a notice to the reader, who will therefore not be led astray. "There is," says La Gorce, in the preface to his *Histoire religieuse de la Révolution française*, "the impartiality born of indifference. That one I have neither the hope nor the desire to attain, and in narrating the Christian trials of our fathers, I dare not affirm that I felt no heartbeat at their sufferings for the Church and for God. If, at the beginning of this book, I promise to be impassible, I should deceive both others and myself. . . . There is another impartiality, one that consists not in the abdication of personal thought, but in the strict observance of truth; that consists in never altering a fact, even a displeasing one, in never mutilating a text, even a troublesome one, in never knowingly misrepresenting the features of a human soul, were it that of an enemy. Such is the gift of a higher impartiality which I ask God to grant me."

Better perhaps confessions of this sort, which are a warning, than a pledge of equanimity which may prove vain, being in two ways difficult to practise, whether the author, in his heart of hearts, unconsciously and in spite of himself, preserves a feeling for his own people or, on the contrary, afraid of yielding to an inborn disposition, goes to the other extreme, and is harder on them than they deserve. On both sides of the road there are ditches.

To what limit can a swerving from the rule of Lucian, Fénelon, Taine, and so many others be admitted?—for there is a limit. Never to the extent of an undue glorifying of the virtues or successes of one's compatriots nor of a disparaging of others'. All the good that the foreigner, nay, the enemy, deserves must come in, and not only come in but be duly praised. In the same way the national faults and mistakes must not be passed over unnoticed, they must be mentioned and blamed. Where nationality will chiefly appear shall not be in a disproportionate praise of the deeds of one's compatriots, but in a deeper feeling of sorrow when faults of theirs have to be recorded.

Moreover, it will perhaps be understood one day that disproportionate praise "does not pay," and, if not for higher motives, out of sheer interest, it will be discarded. Exaggeration, which is a semi-lie, with a part that is true and a part that is not, is usually soon detected, and the reader in his vexation deducts not only all that is false but a part of what is true. The boaster thus proves the loser.

Within those limits which are the same for all, the authors of American histories have a right to show an American heart. In their writings, compatriots, foreign friends, and foreign foes must have their due, which, as in other countries, they sometimes get, sometimes not. In several of the books enjoying the widest circulation these various elements have occasionally less than their due, occasionally more. A number of works have been blamed for being beyond reason pro-English, or beyond reason anti-English. Some of them certainly cannot be taxed with exaggerating the part of France. In one of the most abundantly used in schools the name of Rochambeau does not appear, which, by the way, is the same in the large volume devoted to the United States in the *Cambridge Modern History* (where, even in the bibliography, the important memoirs of the marshal are omitted). In the same manual Steuben, in whom we take pride, for we sent him and paid for his journey, is extolled in the text, and Lafayette is mentioned in a note; much more space is devoted to a so-called "naval war with France" than to the French participation in the struggle for independence, and so on. In another such manual we are told that the "cheering news" received from France in 1780–1781 was that a loan had been granted to John Laurens. Of that scarcely less cheering news that France had sent an army which had safely landed on American soil, with Rochambeau at its head, not a word. Imagine manuals of the Great War with no General Pershing in them !

When such pains will have been taken by

the historian to include what should be included and exclude the rest, to discover truth and
discard falsehood, to reach the solid rock of
facts, to master the clear style which will follow a perfect image of realities to be presented,
to evolve well-weighed and long-matured conclusions, what will be the use of the work thus
produced? In a fit of morosity morose minds
have in our times answered: "None at all."
According to Wendell Phillips: "History is for
the most part an idle amusement, the day-
dream of pedants and triflers." According to
Fustel de Coulanges: "L'Histoire ne sert à
rien." In which case the final result of such
pains and thought and erudition and art would
be similar to a man's life as described by Mac-
beth:

> "a tale
> Told by an idiot, full of sound and fury,
> Signifying nothing."

But history signifies something, and the
whole life of Fustel himself, entirely devoted
to historical research, is a protest against his
own word.

First, history, conscientious, well written,
causes delight, and no honest delight should
be refused to men. It answers our legitimate

longing for knowing what our ancestors did, what were their troubles, their faults, their merits, their successes. The grandest play is played before us in the grandest theatre, with a number of interludes and by-plays, changes of tone, changes of scene.

Then it has something to teach. Fashionable scepticism has derided of late the worth of the "lessons of history," but no amount of deriding can make those lessons lose their worth. They are most of them simple and general enough, but as they are nevertheless periodically forgotten, it is of use that they be periodically put again before the public, who in the end may possibly take note. This is done by historians. The past teaches us, for example, that unbearable abuses breed revolutions; that a class which no longer justifies its privileges by its services is doomed. Remembering the history of the colonies in the ancient world, Turgot said long before the event: "When colonies become sufficient unto themselves they do what Carthage did, and what some day America will do" (November, 1750). The historical intuition of George Washington caused him to write to Gouverneur Morris, then American Minister to France, his admirable letter of October 13, 1789: "The Revolution which has been effected in France is of so wonderful a nature that the mind can hardly realize the fact. If it ends as our last accounts to the 1st of August predict, that nation will be the most powerful and happy in Europe; but I fear, though it has gone triumphantly through the first paroxysm, it is not the last it has to encounter before matters are finally settled. In a word, the Revolution is of too great a magnitude to be effected in so short a space and with the loss of so little blood." I remember having quoted that letter on receiving the news of the Kerensky bloodless revolution in Russia.

Much of the miscalculations of the Germans in 1914 came from their having been the dupes of their own teachings, according to which the other nations had become, in the course of the last fifty years, so weak, corrupt, and immersed in material interests that they would be unable to resist a determined onslaught or to help each other. A better knowledge and understanding of realities would have spared the world the most cruel catastrophes it has ever been afflicted with.

"Every part of modern history," said Lord

Acton, "is weighty with inestimable lessons that we must learn by experience and at a great price, if we know not how to profit by the example and teaching of those who have gone before us, in a society largely resembling the one we live in."

It would not be accurate to allege that, however, as a matter of fact, those examples have never served; in most countries, instructed by precedents, those at the head of affairs now govern with a higher hand than their predecessors of ages ago.

Another advantage, well pointed out by Daunou, is that history makes a nation aware of its continuity, which is almost as much as to say aware of its existence. In the one of his twenty volumes specially devoted to the *Art of Writing History* (708 pages), Daunou says: "Personality subsists only through remembrances; if an individual, ceaselessly renewed in the elements which compose him, recognizes that he continues the same, it is by preserving the memory of what he has done or felt. The same must be said of a people; its persevering identity supposes in it some knowledge of its progresses or vicissitudes, some vestiges of its annals; it would rather accept or devise fabulous ones than have none. Generations which should glide along without leaving any trace, would follow, without continuing, each other; they must transmit memories in order to form a nation or an aggregation of men which passes through different ages and whose life covers several centuries."

No, history is not a mere frivolous amusement; it has its uses; it is worth the labors of its votaries. It requires much pains, much ingenuity and wisdom, several inborn gifts. It is an art of a very special sort which needs, in order to be adequately practised, a scientific mind. From its very nature proceed the rules historians have to observe, and which have been repeatedly declared in the course of centuries, the chief one being that for the strict maintenance of which the American Historical Association has been founded: *Super omnia Veritas.*

THE INFLUENCE OF GRADUATE INSTRUCTION ON HISTORICAL WRITING

WILBUR C. ABBOTT

THE INFLUENCE OF GRADUATE INSTRUCTION ON HISTORICAL WRITING

SOME fifteen years ago one of the leading historical scholars of the United States, in an address to a learned society, bewailed the fact that "in looking about for writers of history in this country at the present moment, the seeker is met with greater discouragement than would befall him in almost any other path of original research." "The American people," he goes on to say, "are in the midst of a cycle of commercialism. There has not been a time, for many years, at any rate, when scholarship has been so lightly valued in the United States as it is at the present moment. . . . Nowadays the size of the output and not the quality of the production is what attracts attention. The standardization of education, not the making of scholars, is the cry. Let any one turn the matter over in his mind and see if he cannot count the really first-class works of American historical writers within the last twenty-five years, on his fingers; and yet conceive of the number of persons engaged in historical pursuits and the number of books constantly published under the guise of history ! Some day the wheel will turn around; scholarship will again be valued as a national asset, and a new Parkman will arise ! Possibly he may produce only one volume, but if that volume shall be of the quality of the 'Pioneers of France,' it will do more for the cause of educating the plain people and the building up of his own reputation than the printing of documents by the ton or the publication of monographs by the dozen."

Nearly a decade and a half has passed since those words were written, and a new Parkman has not yet appeared. Indeed, if any tendency has developed more than another, it would seem to the pessimist to be rather the printing of documents by the ton and the publication of monographs by the score; the insistence on education instead of scholarship and the neglect of history as a form of literature. It is true that within the past few years we have experienced a revival of universal, if not cosmic, history from the pens of untrained or half-trained historians; we have had a tremendous amount of attention paid to the history of the progress of the human mind from philosophic historians or historical philosophers; we have had an increase in the number and content of text-books, taken by publishers, by the public, and perhaps even by their authors, as serious "history." But the number of fingers required to count the really notable writers of history has not increased.

What is the reason for this; and what can be done about it? There are other explanations than the development of education at the expense of scholarship; reasons beyond even commercialism. They lie in perhaps two directions —the authors and the public—as well as in the nature of history as it was and is conceived. Incredible as it may appear to this generation, there was a time, and not so long ago, when history offered a field for an author's ambitions not only for fame but for fortune. Not even the efforts of Mr. Wells, backed by his enormous reputation in another branch of fiction, were as amply rewarded as those of Macaulay. Parkman—whom Professor Channing singles out—and his contemporaries, Prescott and Motley, to say nothing of Bancroft, actually made money out of history, and good history. Few if any historians proper make money out of history in that measure to-day—only the writers of text-books can pretend to such rewards. Hence men write text-books.

This is a fertile theme, but it does not avail to stress the fact that of the first volume of Gardiner's great work some one hundred and seventy-five copies were sold. It was not without truth that Carl Schurz is reported to have said to an aspiring historian: "Ah, you write history. You must have a patrimony." But the result is obvious. If a man is to write history he must have an income independent of his writing, either private or professional. In consequence, since the historical muse cannot offer her less fortunate votaries a living, they teach, and in that teaching, or its accompaniment, exhaust the energies which some of them might otherwise have devoted to scholarship instead of education.

This, indeed, is not all the story. There remains the altered character of history, upon which the modern critics, who denounce much they do not understand or appreciate, pour out the vials of their wrath. Some—indeed much—of their criticism is valid. "If economics is the dismal science," observed one of the last generation of scholars, "history is and ought to be the dull science." And, apart from that dictum, with which most of us would doubtless disagree, the root of the matter lies in the word science, and the development that it indicates. Historical science, so-called, has succeeded or replaced historical literature. And while one may admit that in its method history should and must be scientific, this need not and ought not prevent its being literary on the side of presentation. Unless it is, it will not be read. If it is not read, it will lose much or most of its value as a guide to thought and action.

How, then, is it possible, or is it possible at all, to bring historical writing again into the field of literature without taking it out of the field of science? How is it possible to make it more readable than, let us say, chemistry or physics?

It may be premised at once that there is no recipe for literary skill. The true historian, like the poet, is born, not made. For those who are "called" to write history, and find that the call is justified by its fruits, there is no recipe needed. On the other hand, one cannot stimulate genius in those who have no genius; and in so far the riddle seems insoluble.

Yet something may be done to encourage

the writing of history which, if not the result of natural inspiration, shall at least be intelligible and interesting to the average reader. One of the ways is this. Ever since the influence of the German school of higher education fell upon this country, for good and ill, it has been apparent that manner has been sacrificed to matter, form to substance. The deadening effect of the dissertation has been obvious in nearly every field which relates to literature, or to clear and logical expression, human interest, or any of those qualities which make an appeal to audiences beyond the bounds of specialists and technical experts.

It may be said that this is no more the concern of history than of biology, that the purpose of history, as that of the other sciences, is to arrive at truth, that there is no more reason why a historical work should be "interesting" than a study in pathology. Yet it is obvious that this begs the question. If history is to be divorced from all connection with public interest, save by the medium of text-books, it will die, or at least fail of its purpose to inform and instruct. That argument need not detain us.

Briefly, then, it seems that a beginning may be made among those younger votaries of history who fill our ranks of graduate students; that their work should be directed not merely to the accumulation of facts, but to the arrangement of those facts in at least reasonably readable form; that their "theses" should be so constructed as to appeal not only to the specialists who pass upon their merits, but to a wider public. It is not certain that even the professional readers of these would not welcome a change from the incredible dreariness of some of these productions, many of which should never be permitted to see the light of print until they are humanized. For it is idle to contend that it is not possible to tell the truth in more agreeable form than some of these productions reveal.

This is no plea for less "scholarly," less "scientific," or less "exhaustive" treatment, still less for "popular" presentation; least of all for relaxation of the investigation, the analysis, and criticism necessary for contribution to truth. It is not an appeal for literary "style," though style is not to be despised as much as it has been by some of our more Dryasdust scholars. It is only that we shall have some insistence on—and perhaps training in—form as well as in method and substance.

To this suggestion as to the direction of our graduate work on slightly different lines, many others can and doubtless will be offered. It is too much to hope that it will produce a Macaulay or a Gibbon, even were that desired. But it may do something to make the writing of a thesis more than a mere perfunctory task useful only as a means of getting a degree. It may even do something to correct the situation which now exists—that only a very small fraction of those who write theses ever write anything else.

To this there is one method of approach so necessary, so obvious, so absolutely essential that it would scarcely seem worth while to mention it were it not so largely, or even in many cases so completely, ignored by graduate teacher and student alike. It is reading history. How many times one hears the question asked in doctor's examinations: "What have you read in this field?" How many times the answer is reeled off—a list of titles, books "consulted," "referred to," "looked into," but not, obviously, read, much less inwardly digested. It is the exception rather than the rule to find that a candidate has read all of the work of even one great historian. "I suppose some one has actually read Gibbon and Macaulay through," once observed a professor of history of some note, "but for my part I have never had time."

In that remark lie the two principal indictments of the system. The one is the relatively slight emphasis placed on reading, the other the confession of a life so busy with details that reading seems impossible for its own sake. "If we can only teach men to read and write," observed a famous Oxford tutor, "we are satisfied." It seems a simple formula, but it involves the elements of education—and much more.

The practical difficulty in our scheme of graduate education is that of time. It is generally reckoned that it takes four to five years for one to achieve the degree of doctor of philosophy in any first-rate university, a period as great as that demanded in medicine, and greater than that usually demanded in law, or theology, or engineering, or other professions. To take enough "courses," to prepare for the dreaded examination, to do the investigation and the writing on a dissertation, even this seems almost too little to the average candidate, who is almost invariably in a state of nervous hurry from at least the beginning of his second year. He has no time for mere reading. He must "get up" "bibliography." He must do the "required reading" in his courses. He must take examinations in them. He must, in too many cases, do a certain amount of teaching or "paper work"—reading the periodical tests in undergraduate courses. He is continually too busy.

Part of this is doubtless good for him; from his work as an assistant, corresponding more or less to clinical work in medicine, he learns part of his trade, the mechanics of teaching, the method of conducting classes, of handling the students and the problems which he must later face. He even acquires a considerable amount of actual information of great value to him in his later work. Part of it is, equally without doubt, weariness to the flesh; it is the price he pays for means to go on with his work. But there is beyond this a measure of nervous hurry, common perhaps to American life, which prevents serious reading, contemplation, thought, reflection—all the things which education is supposed to give as a ripening process.

It is this quality which is partly responsible for his failure later to go on with his "scholarly" work. It is partly this which prevents his "producing." Not all; for it is obvious that a considerable proportion of graduate students have no other goal before them than teaching. With them the economic motive, like that in law and medicine and engineering, is supreme. Nor can one find fault with this, as some have done, if we are to make education a real profession, not a mere form of charity or social service, or whatever it may be called, in the endeavor to find a fine name to cover its low financial rewards.

Beside this, there is the demand from every educational institution for services which are but little if at all related to education in the sense of mental training. These which may be grouped under the common name of "administration," whether of committees on educational policy or athletics or social conditions, or discipline, are necessary, if exaggerated, accompaniments of higher mass-education, intermediate education, and even, it would seem nowadays, of elementary education in the United States. Joined to family cares incident to limited means, to the nervous energy used up in the profession most destructive of nervous energy, there seems little time to read, much less to investigate, least of all to publish. It is not so true in science, but it is eminently true in history. Hence it is little wonder that eighty-five per cent or so of our doctors of philosophy never write anything even as substantial as their doctoral dissertations during the rest of their lives.

In a certain sense this result is one which might reasonably be expected. Relatively few persons have the urge to write; still fewer the spirit of investigation; and even in a selected body like the graduate students in history, it must be evident that many have neither the talents nor the desire to produce history. The greater proportion are content with the extremely useful and honorable work of instruction.

Yet, even so, it would seem that, if these things are true, there ought to be some reform in the method of graduate instruction in history. This should be done not merely for the sake of training writers, who will produce something that the public can and will read, but to insure an outlook not bounded by the comparatively narrow limits of the present requirements for the degree, or even by that of history regarded from a purely scientific and informatory point of view, much less from a pedagogic standpoint of material and method of instruction. There should be room for a broader and deeper conception of the whole matter; and if there is no room, room should be made.

The fundamental difficulty seems to be that while there are plenty of courses in "historical method," in "analysis and criticism," in "problems," in all the scientific side of historical work, there are to be found few or none on the side of presentation. Worse than this, perhaps, even in the seminary work which forms so large a part of the best side of historical instruction, little or no attention is paid to the form of the reports there submitted. All the stress is on the matter, little or none on the manner. Reports are frequently, if not in many cases generally, made "orally"; that is, by often long, diffuse, and rambling discussion of the question set for investigation, not a clear, brief, concise, written statement of the problem, the method of investigation, the materials, and the results obtained.

The whole stress has been laid too much on information and on methods of investigation, too little on presentation. Too little attention

has been paid to choice of subject even. Looking over the products of some schools of instruction, it would almost seem that the subject was of little or no importance, its only object being the training of men in methods of
investigation, irrespective of the interest, the
importance, the possibility of future development, the wider bearing, the real importance
of the work done. It seems to be enough to
have a man go through the process of investigation, to learn how to do it, and to prove to
the satisfaction of his instructors that he can
do it with a certain mechanical skill. If it is
published, as it too often is, it is read by the
proof-reader and perhaps an unfortunate re-
viewer or two, and sinks into the oblivion of a
"series."

It is easy to defend this system on two
grounds. The one is that it is "scientific"; that
it makes no pretense to human interest; that it
is enough to clear up a dark way or a disputed
point in history in the interests of pure truth;
that it is no part of the business of science to
be either "human" or "interesting"; that its
only concern is with the extension of knowledge. The other is that the number of graduate
students is so large, the time available for each

is so small that this wholesale method is the only one possible to meet the demands of the situation. To this there might be added a third: that few of these are capable of anything else; that the most one can hope for is the respectable training of respectable scholars and teachers; and that no system can produce genius or even talent. That must come, if at all, by nature.

To these may be added another argument. It is that the graduate student should do his reading himself; that it is no part of the business of the graduate school to direct what should be a natural impulse on his part; that if he has the proper stuff in him he would do it without a "course" in reading. It may be answered that all our work is arranged— for good and ill—in "courses"; that students naturally follow the system which they find; and that the great historians who have not had the advantages of "courses" in a graduate school have not only done their reading themselves, but they have developed their own system of "analysis and criticism," their own methods of investigation, even acquired their own information and bibliography independently of "courses." The argument against a course of historical reading is, in fact, no stronger than that against all other courses.

It would seem, then, that, our system being what it is, there should be introduced into every graduate school of history, where it does not now exist, a course in historiography required of every candidate for a degree. That course should include a survey of leading English, American, French, and German historical writers, not by lectures but by actual reading from week to week of parts of each of the principal writers, with discussion of their work in the class. It should include also a study of their method of handling materials as illustrated by particular passages and treatment of particular subjects throughout their work, preferably by a prepared term report or year report carefully written out. It should certainly include the reading of a whole work of at least one representative historian. It should stress not so much the method of investigation as that of presentation. It should compare the work of several men in the same field or on the same point or problem, the materials they used, the way in which they handled those materials, even the methods they employed to get the effects which they wished to produce. In short, it should treat of history not as pure science but as literature.

No one could pretend that such a course, however diligently taught and studied, would produce great historical writers. But it would do two things—in practice it has done two things—it would provide the student with a far wider and deeper knowledge and understanding of historical writing than he now possesses, and models for his own efforts; and, even though he never wrote a line of history, it would greatly enrich his teaching. It is no panacea for the shortcomings of present historical instruction. It would, however, unquestionably serve as a simple, practical, and highly useful corrective to the present unbalanced system of graduate instruction. That it would be highly appreciated by the students, the experience of those who have tried it fully confirms. That it would enrich the intellectual equipment of both teachers and taught, there is every reason to know. That it might serve as a stimulus and an inspiration to write history, there is reason to hope; for we learn much by imitation.

This is no plea for "style" in the ordinary sense. It has little in common with those courses in English composition which so disturb some of our colleagues. It has nothing to do with rhetoric. It has only two things in mind. The one is the emphasis on the actual writing of history, which is, after all, the only way in which the truths accumulated by investigation can be brought before the world. The other is that it may serve to humanize what is the most human of all "sciences," if not of the "humanities." And to these may be added the great conclusion: that it is not worth while to write what no one will ever read, that if history is to fulfil its mission it must be read, that if it is to be read it must be readable, and if it is to be readable it must be written for the reader in a form which attracts him. Otherwise history will be divorced from life; and while the establishment of courses in historiography in our graduate schools may not avert this catastrophe; while it may seem a small remedy against a great evil; if the habit of reading and writing can be firmly fixed in the mass of graduate students—to say nothing of undergraduates—it will be one step toward the humanizing of the whole field.

For that, after all, has been the root of the whole matter. History in the hands of ultra-specialists has been too largely dehumanized. The danger lies not on the side of investigation; there the scientific spirit cannot be too strongly urged. But there has been a powerful tendency to inject the scientific method into presentation. There is no essential or fundamental truth in dulness; there is no reason why truth should not be interesting. There is no reason why it cannot be made interesting without ceasing to be true.

Finally, there is one curious phenomenon which, were there no other argument for this point of view, seems to prove it true. It is the fact that outside the realm of historical instruction and scholarship in the usual sense there have arisen so many well-known, widely read histories written by all sorts of men who find in history their medium of expression. And more—they have received from historical scholars themselves that meed of attention, even of praise, which these same scholars are apt to deny to the duller men of their own craft. They criticise—but they read! Is it not time they applied this lesson to their own circle of influence, and tried, in so far as possible, to infuse their own students with some of the qualities they approve in these writers of history outside the pale of "trained historians"?

It is these books which they put in the hands of their students—at least, their undergraduate students—rather than the learned monographs. The same is true of the world in general. The history it reads is for the most part not written by historical scholars proper, trained in "schools" of historical instruction. It is not the kind where "furious footnotes growl 'neath every page." Scholars write for each other, not for the public. They are afraid of each other; for they have, what the non-professional "historian" has not, a professional reputation as historical scientists at stake, and to them the most minute discrepancy in fact is of far more importance than unreadability.

It may be urged again that this is no mere matter of a "brilliant style." It is merely telling the story which they have to tell in clear, straightforward language, so that it may be read and understood by any one without too great extinction of boredom. It is a matter of logical arrangement—so often lacking in those masses of undigested material called theses. It is a matter of thinking things out, of selection and arrangement, which, after all, can be taught. It is a matter of time. For to many a graduate student the time spent on presentation bears no relation to that spent on investigation. One must not expect Macaulays and Gibbons to grow on every graduate-school bush; but it is worth while to read the story of how the former sought the right word or expression to clothe his thought, as it is written in Trevelyan, or to reflect that the latter rewrote the first chapter of the *Decline and Fall* six times. One may consider as well the observation of Thucydides that his great history was not written as a prize essay.

This is no plea that the time spent on the investigation of the facts shall be in any measure minimized, only that the time spent on presentation shall not be scamped, or even eliminated, as it too often is. It is no insistence on "style" as style, nor any argument for the subordination of matter to manner. But in the eternal triangle of history, science, and literature, the historic muse has spent too much time with the former and too little with the latter. One hates to think—viewing many of the reports and theses which pass before his eyes—that the style is the man himself. That is too depressing for the future of historical scholarship in America. He prefers to believe that were more attention paid to form, the whole of historical scholarship would be benefited. For history is no mere accumulation of facts; it is not masses of notes and information; it is not the product of a "lifetime of horrid industry" alone. It requires more than the ability to read endless volumes and manuscripts and make endless references. It requires thought. It needs the mind as well as the eye and hand. Without thought it is but sounding brass and tinkling cymbal, out of tune and harsh. Without informing ideas it becomes a chaos without form and void.

So that, if this is to be avoided, it is necessary to train the mind as well as the eye and memory, to emphasize ideas as well as facts, clearness as well as accuracy, logic as well as industry. It is necessary, above all, to recognize that manner has some place, not as literary style but as the expression of mentality, that quality rather than quantity is the test of ability, and intelligence as well as patience an element of history. We may not, and we must not, expect that the "penetration of genius" shall take the place of scientific investigation. But we have a right to expect that imagination and—it has been urged—even hypothesis shall have the place in history which they have in great science. We have a duty to encourage originality as well as profundity; even, perhaps, to give generalization a place beside minute particularization. There is danger in this, as in everything worth while; but it is the risk which everything worth while must run. Finally, it is important that the most human and in some ways the most interesting of all subjects shall not have its humanity and its interest crushed out by the weight of pseudo-scientific elimination of all human interest. For, after all, it was men who made history, and the greatest of historians have been the most human.

Finally, it is obvious that there are two dangers in such a plan as this. The first is that it may be interpreted in terms of lectures on the work of different historians, a formal exercise illuminated, if at all, only by "prescribed reading." The second is that it may give rise to a mistaken belief, that mere reading makes a historian, that, as in so many other departments of life and learning, dilettante dallying over the work of others, "appreciation," criticism, and their attendant sprites may take the place of investigation, that words may be regarded as work. For it is necessary to be doers of the word, not hearers only; and it is so much easier to point out where Macaulay falls short, and the method of Thucydides is inadequate, where Motley is out of date, and Taine was prejudiced, than it is to write anything worth while one's self. If there is anything good in historical training in our universities, it is not making models of universal superficiality or even mere critics. It is first to see that one shall know as much about a little piece of history as any one else in the world—or more; that he can himself, on occasion, actually produce something worth while; and that he shall have as sound a knowledge and judgment about the rest as time and Providence vouchsafe him. Somewhere between the minute dulness of the confirmed historical microscopist and the glittering generalities of the confirmed historical smatterer there lies a golden mean; somewhere between the rhetorician and the scholiast lies a safe road. For the first requisite of writing history is knowing some history to write, not merely having some agreeable ideas on it; and the second is actually writing it, not throwing it together.

THE CRAFTSMANSHIP OF THE HISTORIAN
CHARLES W. COLBY

THE CRAFTSMANSHIP OF THE HISTORIAN

IT is a long way from Herodotus to the late Robert Flint, author of *A History of the Philosophy of History*. The Ægean is not so distant from the Forth as are these writers from each other. Merely to mention their names is to disclose the universe over which historiography extends. The father of the art tells his story in the common speech of his contemporaries—setting up for all time a standard of lucid, graphic narrative. The Scottish professor, likewise an historian, is constrained by the nature of his subject to use terms which bring us inside the frontier of metaphysics. Can it be doubted that Flint would have made Herodotus stare and gasp?

Many other illustrations could be used to show what is involved when we begin to discuss the writing of history. Consider, for example, the incalculable number of books which have been written regarding different aspects of the past. Without trying to be statistically precise, let any one make his own guess regard-

ing the number of historical works which will
be found in three collections only—the Biblio-
thèque Nationale, the British Museum, and
the Library of Congress. For present purposes
it does not matter whether these are numbered
by hundreds of thousands or millions. The
broad fact is that for many centuries, in many
lands, historians of all sorts and conditions
have sought to record events in some sort of
order. Just as the stranger who traverses sub-
alpine Italy for the first time is overwhelmed
by fatigue in contemplating the stone walls
which have been piled up through the appal-
ling industry of former generations, so it is with
the historian who turns back to contemplate
what has been wrought by his predecessors.
Such an accumulation of books, written in
such a variety of styles !

But it is not merely through a sharp contrast between individual historians, or through
a statistical enumeration of existing histories
that we are made to realize the complexities by
which we are beset when we start out to clarify
our thought regarding the problem of historical composition. We come to grips with the
subject only when we apply the old touchstone
of *quidquid agunt homines*. What limit is pos-

sessed by history save the whole scope of human thought and action? There is no phase of life in times past which does not furnish a legitimate theme to the historian. Taking this axiom for a point of departure, let those of an analytical habit enumerate all the categories of man's endeavor. Having thus reached a very large figure, consider further the number of angles which each of these subjects possesses when contemplated by the minds of different investigators. Multiplying the number of categories by the number of angles, one reaches a result which would not seem contemptible even in the field of astronomical mathematics. And, at least theoretically, it is only in the light of some such final figure that we can attempt to map out the whole potential field of historical composition. An indefinite multitude of subjects approached by a still larger multitude of minds must yield a crop of literary compositions which will present an infinite variety of aspect.

Considered thus, the writing of history is a subject that should not be approached save in a mood of pious agnosticism. But as often happens, the practical difficulties of a problem are less acute than those suggested by a theoretical view of it. Having contemplated the more than Minoan labyrinth of historical composition as a whole, let us look around for a thread which, though it will not lead us through every back alley of the maze, may at least bring us out into the daylight. The clew suggested is simply this, that in a high percentage of cases historical essays, pamphlets, and books would be written better than they are at present if their authors would take the trouble to write as well as they can. In other words, the failure of the average historian to write well is due less to invincible ignorance or congenital disability than to laches. He would do much better if he but took the trouble.

Reviewing the whole field of historical literature, it becomes clear that no trouble is wasted which brings the historian up to his highest level as a writer. To dispraise one's predecessors is very unpleasant, and it is irksome even to seem to dispraise them. Yet the paucity of great historians is an inescapable fact—whether the matter be considered absolutely or relatively. For almost two thousand five hundred years the writing of histories has been a common practice, and has assumed that wide variety of forms to which reference has been made already. On the whole, the histories which deal with politics and war have flourished the most riotously; but no broad domain of human effort has been neglected. Theology, art, literature, science, music, commerce, exploration are no more than a few among the leading categories of man's activity which have been chronicled in copious detail. There is also that fascinating record of individual achievement which we call biography. Dividing and subdividing, the number of histories seems endless. And yet there have been few great historians.

Buckle was impressed by this fact, for at the very beginning of his *History of Civilization* he refers to the whole body of historical writing in terms of extreme disparagement. Casting about for a reason which will explain its shortcomings, he first states that almost no one of real creative power—at least no one of the highest mentality—has condescended to write histories. Here he has in mind the monumental intelligences like Kepler and Newton. He does remember that Francis Bacon wrote a history of the reign of Henry VII, but neglects to observe that the eminent Leibnitz stooped to compile the annals of a German principality.

Following Buckle, one must conclude painfully that historians are not equal in mental power to philosophers and physicists; in fact, that they do not rank among the thinkers. Nor is he alone in this opinion. Gibbon, by common consent, is a giant among historians. Yet Sir James Macintosh said that you could snip Gibbon's mind off a corner of Burke's without removing enough to be noticeable.

/ Admitting the infrequency of great historians, there would seem to be a much better explanation of this phenomenon than that offered by Buckle. The reason why histories of the highest class are so few is not necessarily to be discovered in lack of intellectual power among historians. It would be much more accurate to say that no one can be a complete, well-rounded historian without possessing gifts and qualities which are rarely found in combination. By enumerating some of these it may be possible to show the relation which the writing of history holds to the completed work.

That the historian may achieve real eminence, he must possess a mind which is clear enough to seize upon a suitable subject and wide enough to view it in due perspective. The theme chosen must be of considerable proportions, though not so large as to be overwhelming. In dealing with it the historian must possess such a degree of intellectual detachment as will insure fairness; yet he must not be so detached as to become colorless. He must possess a robust and unquenchable sympathy with mankind, without being a sentimentalist. He must have a zeal for his task which will make him willing to scorn delights and live laborious days. Many years he must pass in libraries, being his own pedant before he can put life into his pages. His spirit must be calm, yet eager. And though he be perfect in all these respects, one thing more is necessary. He must know how to write so that the world will read. How this can be achieved it may seem futile to inquire. A very few can do it; the rest fail.

Let us not, however, follow the line of least resistance in assuming that it is futile to inquire whether improvement cannot be made in the writing of history as practised by the many. "It takes two to speak truth," says Thoreau; "one to speak and one to listen." For this reason the pre-eminent historian must employ a style which will command a wide audience. It may be thought niggardly or unjust to deny the title of greatness to the historian who, with conspicuous ability, monumental learning, and exemplary fairness, produces an *opus* that is designed for scholars only. Everything depends on definition. At the same time no argument is needed to demonstrate that those who, besides being learned, can write strongly, must stand higher on the bead-roll of select historians than those who are unable to emerge beyond the muniment room.

Sir Walter Raleigh—of Oxford—has left us several apothegms connected with college examinations, in one of which he observes that the king who made all his subjects dukes was an anarchist. Following this precept, the number of leaders in any department of endeavor can be but small, and among historians the few whose works command wide attention throughout the ages survive because they possessed the power to communicate their personality through words. For us the point is that we should not dismiss the matter with a phrase about the miracle of genius. Rather should we note with care how a faculty for expression has given the masters of our art their distinctive place—style proving to be the *porro unum necessarium.* Not every one who pursues an art can become a master, but it is possible for every one to aim at being an artist rather than an artisan.

It would be a short cut out of the difficulty if one could say with truth that in times past the high mortality among histories has been due to a wilful neglect of the literary vehicle. But no such statement as this could be made with truth if it pretended to cover the whole period during which histories have been written. In a notable percentage of cases much more attention has been paid to the style than to the content—witness so many of the works which were published during the age of rococo and baroque architecture. In part this was a time of genuine erudition, but it also abounded with writers who were chiefly concerned to win reputation with as little fatigue as possible; namely through the help of rhetoric. The lamentable circumstance is that so often the real scholar has been content to collect an excellent mass of building-materials without attempting to use them himself, or in attempting to use them has put forth an effort by no means comparable to the value of his materials. Whether broken down by the toil of research or complacent because he had settled Hoti's business, he

has failed too often to plan his time so that at
the end his work would show evidences of de-
sign. It is true that there are some great scholars who would find it impossible to write an
effective narrative or interpretation, even if
they strove to do so; but these constitute a
small minority, however important.

One can easily compile, of course, a list of
historians who took themselves and their writings very seriously. Thucydides, with his κτῆμα
ἐς αἰεί, is the classical example of the master
who aimed high and succeeded. Much lower
down on the list is Gregory of Tours, making
his deep appeal to the sympathy of later ages
when he adjures the future scribe not to tam-
per with his text—"no, not even though he has
all the learning of Martianus!" Centuries later
Maximilien de Béthune, Duc de Sully, vindicated the dignity of history with all his might
by putting on court dress when he engaged in
the composition of those memoirs which he
wrote in the second person. Illustrations of this
character can be multiplied without impairing
the force of the broad statement that over a
long period the writing of history has suffered
because the truly erudite have taken less pains
than they ought to have taken when they set

out to communicate the results of their studies. Here, however, we are concerned with the writing of history as a practical matter in our own day. Without attempting further to comment upon the broader or more distant aspects of the subject, let us review some of the conditions which have affected historiography during the past fifty or seventy-five years— that is to say, within recent memory, as historians reckon time.

The older members of our association were taught, in large part, by men imbued with what has often been called the scientific conception of history. Without attempting to define this in exact terms, it may be recalled that during the last quarter of the last century all reputable historians were engaged in clearing away a vast rubbish of ignorance, prejudice, and misrepresentation. To them it seemed that earlier historians had been partisans, and that even where they had been sincere, their methods of investigation were very imperfect. Accordingly, it was a pre-eminent duty to conduct research in the spirit of the biologist, the chemist, and the physicist. One of the most important executives in New York has placed in full view over the entrance to his office a placard

which reads: "What are the Facts?" He feels
sure that it has saved him a great deal of time.
Now, forty or fifty years ago all historians of
the pure sect were asking this same question,
to the exclusion of almost every other: "What
are the Facts?"

The reason why this query was then so
urgent is very manifest, since such a vast mass
of inaccuracy had become lodged in the public
consciousness during the preceding uncritical
period. How urgent the need was can only be
realized by those who have taken the trouble
to read the polemical literature that extends
from Middleton's *Free Inquiry* to the days
when the *Quarterly Review* was denouncing
"the absurd and shallow doctrines of Nie-
buhr." It meant a real struggle to rout the
forces of obscurantism and make it possible
for the light to be let in.

Remembering this conflict, we can sympa-
thize with the pioneers who strove for enlight-
enment at the time when criticism was equiv-
alent to heresy. This date, however, is long
past, and at present it may not be unwise to
consider whether the full triumph of critical
and comparative methods does not in its turn
disclose fresh conditions. The controlling pur-

pose, one may contend, under which data should be chosen, combined, and presented, is no less a factor now than it was in those long ages before the net of criticism had swept in everything from Ranofer and Khafre to the *Legend of Marcus Whitman*. Three generations have elapsed since Ranke began his career with *The History of the Romance and German Races;* the Ecole des Chartes has been publishing its journal ever since 1839; and it was in 1863 that Droysen opened the ninth volume of the *Historische Zeitschrift* with his paper on the *Elevation of History to the Rank of a Science*. The fruits of critical research are abundant and magnificent; yet criticism is not everything here below, and some of its by-products have taken form in tendencies which need to be corrected.

The scientific historian employing the critical method has often worked in the spirit of a sectarian. Reacting strongly from slipshod investigation and special pleading, he took it for his task to discover and set forth the truth. His own temper was to be one of severe impartiality—"the disinterestedness of the dead," as Lord Acton put it. But being human, he could not deny himself wholly the joys of combat.

It became his delight to unmask time-honored myths—winning renown or deriving satisfaction through an enlargement of the borders of knowledge. In a letter to Freeman, Green expresses admiration of Gardiner, and can quite understand why, striving as he does to banish "loose talk," he should look askance at the influence which the *Short History* might have in bringing it back again. Not only during the seventies, but during the eighties and nineties was "loose talk" frowned upon by historians of approved nurture. The great objective was to secure results by knocking some one's eye out; that is to say, by disproving an old view through proving a new one.

Let us grant that this habit of mind is one with which no fault can be found save where it runs to extremes; but throughout the last quarter of the last century the desire to stimulate intensive research got somewhat out of bounds. While labor was lavished upon the work of preparation, the researcher permitted his "results" to be presented on paper with slight regard to proportion and phrasing. For the time being, at least, the equipoise had been upset and the writing of history suffered because it was assumed that whenever the his-

torian grew animated, interesting, or picturesque, he ran into the grievous sin of talking
loosely. Most people have minds which run on
a single track. In the present instance it is
suggested that the zeal for accuracy and impartiality, which has added so much of late
to the value of historical studies, carries with
it a danger; for it is a real danger if preoccupation with new facts established or new theories vindicated renders the historian indifferent
to the form in which they are presented.

Another mode of approach is to recognize
that every one who writes about the past is
faced by two tasks—the critical and the syn-
thetic. Coming first in the sequence of effort,
the task of criticising materials and sifting
data may well prove too engrossing or ex-
hausting if it is not recognized that when
this part of the work has been finished an
equally grave duty remains. Nothing is easier
or more exhilarating than to set up noble
standards for other people, but it would be
begging the question were one not to urge that
the historian, besides collecting facts, must use
and shape them. Confessedly, in many cases
the scope for artistic treatment will not be
great. Historical literature, however else it

may be divided, falls naturally into two broad classes—the chronological and the interpretative. The authors of *L'Art de Vérifier les Dates* thought very little about style as a means of appealing to the judgment or the emotions. It is the same with writers of monographs which are so limited in purpose that they pretend to do nothing but present an accurate catalogue of facts which occurred at certain times and places. For present purposes, books of this character may be dismissed as chronologies rather than histories, though even here there is a clear distinction between good and bad in respect to arrangement and statement. The moment we pass beyond the department of chronology, the historian becomes a writer no less than an investigator. If he evades the responsibility which is implied by this statement, he is condemning himself to sterility. In most cases he labors because he wishes to be useful rather than to amuse himself. And how can he be useful—except within very narrow limits— if he will not take the trouble to write as well as he can?

And there is need to write well when the historian selects a subject which requires real power of thought. One kind of talent is required to collect the data; another kind of talent is required when the story comes to be told, whether as plain narrative or with interpretative comment. So long as the historian is content to keep within the limits of a strict chronological summary, he may not cause disappointment if his style is without color or quality. Here he is dealing in a narrow way with what has been ascertained beyond question—like the date of the battle of Waterloo. But when he mounts to those higher levels where abide the souls of great men, the seeds of great movements, and the mysteries of racial development, he loses contact with what is certain and enters a region where the sole criterion is probability. Hence to enforce his convictions he must become a pleader who depends for his effect upon the arrangement of his brief and the selection of his words. The scientific historian is often afraid of danger the moment he ceases to be colorless. He should be less timid. No one denies to Darwin the title of scientist, and in his autobiography he says that the *Origin of Species* is one long argument. Likewise the element of argument enters into every historical book which is modelled on large lines. To make his work convincing, shapely, admirable, the historian must let his own mind and nature shine through it—at their best. This he will not and cannot do unless he grasps the fundamental conception that the duty to write well can no more be disregarded than the duty to research well.

In most cases a much higher standard of expression could be reached were it not for perverse neglect. To illustrate this statement, let us consider the specific example which is afforded by the contrast between J. H. Wylie's *History of England under Henry the Fourth* and the *Ford Lectures on the Council of Constance* delivered at Oxford by the same author. This contrast is rendered the more striking by the four pages entitled "L'Envoi" with which the *Ford Lectures* are brought to a close.

Like Matthew Arnold, J. H. Wylie was an inspector of schools, but here the resemblance would be thought to cease by any one who turned suddenly from Arnold's *Essays* to Wylie's *History of England under Henry the Fourth*—a work of much learning, but wholly without literary allurement. The significant fact is that having lavished years of effort upon four volumes which are marked by an aggressive baldness of style, Wylie produced on the

Council of Constance a little book that scintillates with cleverness. Obviously it is impossible to quote here long passages illustrating the dulness of the work on Henry IV or the liveliness of the *Ford Lectures,* but attention must be called to the terms in which Wylie comments upon his critics. There have been few wittier valedictories. Wylie's "L'Envoi" is not long, and it is so germane to the present discussion that no apology need be made for quoting it without abridgment:

"In bringing this course of lectures to a close I may perhaps be allowed to finish with a personal note. So far as I am able to judge, the reason why the University of Oxford has done me the honor to invite me to deliver the course is probably due to the fact that I have spent a great many years of what some would call hard labor in producing one solitary historical book. While many critics have dealt leniently with it, to others it has proved a source of exasperation on account of its overminuteness and its want of literary style. Both are grave faults in any author who wishes to command popularity, and I can only defend myself by saying that the book in question was purely the work of an amateur, written with

the sole aim of securing thoroughness so far as
it lay in my power, and that I have to that extent respected my public that I have striven
to supply it not with pleasure but with food.

"To begin with the second charge, the want
of style. There is no doubt that Literature is
Art and Art is Selection, and that the writer
who cannot select with nicety is neither an
artist nor a litterateur. Yet I am consoled with
the knowledge that your great constitutional
historian, Bishop Stubbs, once said of his own
work that the useful part of it was hard reading and the readable part 'trifling,' which
would soon 'go the way of all fireworks.' But,
after all, the style, the art that carries all by
storm and wins along the whole line, is a God-
given gift. Those who have it cannot fail to
make it felt, while those who have it not would
do well to make no effort to affect it, remembering that even a DeRougemont [may be
found out at last, for all his gift of imagination. So in the matter of style I can only feel
that it must just be left as it is. That which we
are, we are, and there is no use in trying to be
anything else.

"But on the other horn—of over-minute-
ness—I am prepared to make a momentary

stand. Over-anything is, of course, a fault, and μηδὲν ἄγαν is a rule beyond reproach. But minuteness, if not *over*-minute, is not a malady from which history-writing has suffered in the past, and I am pleased to think that with all its drawbacks, its day is only just beginning. As knowledge grows, the *Weltgeschichte* and *Histoire Universelle* becomes more and more impossible. The effort that was once put forth to range over a continent is now barely sufficient to master the biography of a single home. We all know the old methods of the eighteenth century; character sketches and fancy portraits, Thucydidean in scope and drawn to display the wordy skill of the draughtsman; lofty and often contradictory generalizations, all based upon the same meagre stock of knowledge; a modicum of well-worn facts tricked out in varying degrees of picturesqueness. Indeed, after many years of minute reading, I am almost constrained to say that I know nothing sadder in literature than the way in which old fictions are repeated by favorite authors without any attempt at verification from original sources.

"But whether we like it or not, we have certainly now passed into what has been called

'the documentary age,' which was recently
forecast as 'destined to develop learning at
the expense of writing, and to make history independent of historians,' and (shall I add) lec-
turees independent of lectur*ers*. This may not
be a cheering outlook, but it should be remembered that to our forefathers Rymer's *Fœdera*
was a revelation; yet it put fresh life into the
treatment of the whole field of English history,
and did not in the end destroy the delight of
students any more than the discovery of the
Assyrian bricks or the Moabite stone, and if
we test and prove and spare no pains in reverence for our subject there should be no fear for
the result, either in regard to the enjoyment of
the students or the progress of the study.

"The Oxford Historical Society was once
bravely told that 'dulness is dreadful,' but
that 'there are worse things than dulness—
worse if that which professes to be history is
no history at all.' And therefore it is something
to know from recent pronouncements on the
future of historical inquiry that henceforward
our backs are to be ruthlessly turned on the old
barren generalizations, and that we are to look
on no detail as trivial which tends to supple-
ment our scanty knowledge of the past. So if

the method of the minute researcher does not yet commend itself as too quixotic to be practicable, he must just be content to take a lowly place for the present, consoled with the knowledge that he sometimes catches out the high-flyer and obtains occasional recognition in some quarter where he least expected it."

After reading this vindication—and the *Ford Lectures* as a whole—one can only regret that J. H. Wylie did not display in his four volumes on Henry IV the literary talent which he possessed. He is hoist with his own petard. With respect to writing, his main contention is that "the style, the art that carries all by storm and wins along the whole line, is a God-given gift. Those who have it cannot fail to make it felt, while those who have it not would do well to make no effort to affect it." But surely it is not a question of extremes, with no middle point between Thucydides and Dryasdust. Doctor Holmes once had an experience with a printer's devil which led him ever after to refrain from being as funny as he could. But the historian is not relieved from the obligation of writing as well as he can. In Wylie's case the *Ford Lectures* prove that it was well within his power to attract readers and hold them. Had he displayed the same quality in his elaborate work on Henry IV, his long labors would have been of far greater utility to others. It is wholly improper for the historian to say that because he cannot write like Thucydides he will not strive to write well.

Public opinion counts for much in these matters, and if historians of eminence believe that something should be done about it, the level of historical writing can and will be raised. There is no short cut to the production of masterpieces, nor will there be until some way is discovered to produce great men. Manifestly the genius takes care of himself. But measured by number, an infinitesimal fraction of the histories published in a given generation bear the marks of genius or of a talent which approaches it. Multitudes of histories are called for and will be written. If attention is concentrated on methods of research and the necessity of producing "results," these new books are not likely to differ very much from those which have been written during the past forty years. On the other hand, a searching of heart among the guides of opinion might lead to some betterment.

A like subject was discussed long ago by

Matthew Arnold in his essay on *The Literary Influence of Academies.* "How much better," he exclaims, "is the journeyman work of literature done in France than in England!" The explanation is that through the Academy, France possesses a standard—or, rather, a sense of standard—which is lacking in England. The French do not write merely as the spirit listeth, but with the express recognition of the fact that there is such a thing as form or shapeliness.

Applying this analogy to the present case, there exists throughout the English-speaking world that important force which is exercised through the universities. While their authority is not precisely that of the French Academy, their influence is wide and pervasive. Now with hardly an exception all those who teach history in the leading universities of the United States are members of the American Historical Association. It follows that any effort which had the strong support of the Association would also receive the support of the universities. The Association has felt enough interest in the writing of history to appoint a Committee. It may conclude, after considering the Committee's report, that nothing can be done beyond the expression of pious aspirations. On the other hand, it may feel moved to attempt some form of concerted action.

Proceeding by elimination, let us consider what scope there is for concerted action. To begin with, no member of the Committee possesses such hardihood as would be required from one who would dare dogmatize to the senior historians. Men fifty years old have learned how to write or they never will learn. Furthermore, they would be justified in taking umbrage at the suggestions offered to them by a committee for their own guidance. Extreme courtesy might prevent them from saying anything aloud, but to themselves they would say: "Go to!—Who are you, to tell us how we should write our books!" But candidates for the degree of Doctor can be addressed with less embarrassment, and it is not impossible that for them the Association can do something practical. Let us assume that there exists a benevolent intention. How can it be made to take form?

In the first place, certain broad conceptions must be enforced upon the consciousness of the younger historians by their seniors—if the seniors feel that they can speak with conviction. Some of these may be enumerated as follows:

1. In range, historical writings are of the utmost diversity—extending from bald digests of fact to works of generalization which impinge upon metaphysics.

2. Corresponding to this diversity of subject, there is and must always be a wide variation in treatment. A chronological digest is one thing; an effort to disclose motive or portray events picturesquely is something quite different. And each calls for an appropriate style.

3. Giving due weight to these categorical distinctions, the fact remains that all too often historians devote far less care to the task of literary presentation than should be devoted to it. While the gift of style is possessed by few, the value of most historical works would be increased if their authors tried seriously to express themselves with impact.

4. Enthusiasm for research should not be suffered to become overweening. The young researcher, like the young diplomatist, should guard himself against excess of zeal. Obviously, materials must be collected and sifted first of all. But when the facts have been mastered, it still remains to write the thesis or the book—

a task quite different in character, yet so exacting that failure therein minimizes the value to others of the work as a whole.

5. A due relationship must be observed between the energy devoted to research and the energy devoted to writing. It is a question of maintaining the equipoise. If the young historian is suffered to believe that history is a science only, he becomes the victim of a one-sided conception. A generation ago it was important, indeed indispensable, to point out that loose generalizations are not substitutes for knowledge. Now the problem of synthesis is clamoring for attention, and, as the greater includes the less, synthesis includes writing.

It is true that statements like these, when itemized, look like a string of platitudes. None the less, a platitude is often a *neglected* truth. If the leaders of opinion in matters relating to history will but stress the importance of the considerations just summarized, there is a strong probability that the younger historians will devote somewhat more attention to writing than they have devoted to it hitherto.

A concluding suggestion is that a course on historiography should be included in the curriculum of every university which has resources enabling it to conduct advanced work. The subject-matter is such that a course of this character could be made extremely stimulating. Indeed, its influence ought to extend far beyond the domain of style, phrasing, and modelling.

These suggestions are based upon the belief that the American Historical Association can do something for the writing of history, if its members feel that the subject is one which merits and demands attention. It is hardly too much to hope that should a genuine conviction be found to exist among the seniors, means will be discovered to voice it in such wise as to arrest the attention of those historians who are now serving their apprenticeship. Personal influence would accomplish much. Personal influence supported by systematic instruction would accomplish more.

THE PRESENT STATE OF HISTORY-WRITING

JOHN SPENCER BASSETT

THE PRESENT STATE OF HISTORY–WRITING

A S this report is being written the American Historical Association is completing the first forty years of its existence, a comparatively brief period in the life of a great cultural society, but nevertheless a period rich in progress and actual achievements. In 1884 the big universities had one or two professors of history where they now have ten or more. Most colleges had one professor of history, but he usually taught it in connection with political economy, political science, or public speaking. To-day the average college has from two to five teachers of history, and political economy and political science have been made separate departments. Forty years ago history was taught in a perfunctory manner in the public schools; now it has a strong place in the grades and in the high school. In university, college, and public schools, as compared with 1884, history is now being taught several times more in quantity and several times better in method.

With this brilliant advance we have a right to expect history to be in a better position with the men and women of the country than ever before. Since more of them have studied it in school, ought we not to expect that a very large part of our people should be interested in reading history, that a great demand should exist for historical books, and that a large and powerful group of historians should be writing many histories to meet this demand? But no such conditions exist. From the librarians who hand out the books which the people read, from the publishers and booksellers who distribute the books that are published, and from all other competent observers of actual conditions comes unvarying testimony that history is less read to-day than formerly, and that it is not in strong demand at this time with the people we are accustomed to call the "educated class." Such was not the case forty years ago.

The attention of the writer was pointedly called to this situation a few years ago on reading a circular received from a popular "literary agency," whose business was to find markets for articles whose authors could not dispose of them without assistance. This particular circular, after enumerating many kinds of writings that were salable, said with brief emphasis: "But no history is wanted." It is possible that the writer of the circular had some pique against history, and his pique may have been responsible for the curt respect he paid the subject; but it is not to be doubted that his business instinct would have made him willing to take historical writing to sell, if he had thought it possible to sell it.

Here is another indication of the same change in the attitude of the public. Forty years ago history had a place in the magazines. Witness the series of articles on the Civil War published in *The Century Magazine*, and later brought out in four large volumes with the title, *Battles and Leaders of the Civil War*. Such a series would sink any magazine to-day. I find that in 1884 the *Century* published twenty articles that may be said to have been historical, *Harper's Magazine* published twenty-one, and *The Atlantic Monthly* published twenty-two. Let the reader turn to these same periodicals for 1924 and see how many historical articles appeared in them in that year.

Every well-wisher of history is doubtless concerned to know the reasons why this vast amount of history-studying has not led to a wider popular interest in the subject studied. It is the writer's purpose to examine the methods and aims of the older group of historians, to contrast with them the methods and aims of the new school, to discuss the influence of the methods of the new school on historical style, to point out some of the undesirable habits into which our writers have fallen, and to offer the testimony of some persons whose experience qualifies them as experts in the situation. It is not to be expected that any one person can lay down rules for others to follow. But it is not too much to hope that the readers, and especially the younger men and women who are giving themselves to history, may be incited to make an examination of the subject, each according to his or her individual needs. For there is no single road in which all feet may walk. Each man goes as his own nature makes possible; and it matters not how he goes, if his steps lead to the achievement of the best in him.

In considering the development of history in the period under discussion, it is necessary to point out the relation between style and some of the characteristics of the present school of history. It may even seem that in condemning the effects which some of the current practices exert on style, the writer is condemning the practices themselves. He does not mean to condemn them. He merely writes, as he sees it, of the situation that has come about. He would be pleased if the situation proved to be brighter than it is here painted.

Moreover, nothing that occurs here is intended to express dispraise for the splendid gains to history due to the arrival of the so-called scientific spirit in history. The value of detachment, criticism of evidence, dependence on original sources, and devoted examination of every available source in order to arrive at the truth, these are priceless things and they can never be relinquished. They have to do with the content of history, and in that sense they are the essentials of the new school. Our business is with the form in which the new school expresses itself, and style and content must be kept distinct in the mind of the reader, although in the discussion it may sometimes appear that they are not as truly distinct as can be desired. Much as we might like to recover the pleasant manner of writing of the old school, it would be regained at too high a cost if it meant discarding the recent gains in spirit and content.

HISTORIANS BEFORE 1884

Speaking broadly, it is convenient to take the year in which the American Historical Association was founded as the dividing point between the old and new schools of history. This organization was so completely a product of the new spirit then moving in our profession, and it has so completely dominated the field since it was founded, that its creation may be taken as the time at which the new ideas took the lead over the old. It is true that the men who brought in the new spirit were active before 1884, and it is also true that most of the men of the old school came willingly into the Association; but speaking roughly, it is not possible to point to a date earlier than 1884 at which it can be said that the new prevailed, nor to a date much later than 1884 at which it can be said that the old school was still in the ascendant.

Before this notable year, then, the historians in the United States may be ranged in three classes. First were a small number of distinguished writers whose books were received with great favor by the intelligent public on account of their accepted ideas and agreeable style. Among them the best were Bancroft, Prescott, Motley, and Parkman, men not equally great nor esteemed by the public in proportion to their excellence. Making due allowance for the shifting standards of the times, their fame continues to this day.

In the second we may place a number of industrious and conscientious writers, less known than the members of the first group, because they worked in restricted fields. They were earnest in the cause of history and gave us books of real value. Among them can be placed Charles Gayarré, J. R. Brodhead, Henry C. Murphy, Edward B. O'Callaghan, Gilmary Shea, John G. Palfrey, Henry Onderdonk, Jr., Gabriel Furman, and others of worth and local fame. Most of us living to-day have never known the works of such men, or if known we have forgotten them. But in their own times they had firm recognition and most of them are still held in great esteem in their own communities.

Into the third class may be put a large number of delvers into the past, men who discovered hidden facts in small things and set them down with zeal and joy. They were interested in the "antiquities" of places, in the details of battles, in genealogical phases of history, or in the remains of the early settlers. Men like these gave life to *The Historical Magazine*, which the devoted but peppery Henry B. Dawson edited for many years, and lengthened the days of *The Magazine of American History*, which Mrs. Martha J. Lamb kept alive by many sacrifices until she finally died at her post in 1893.

The characteristics of the old school may be stated as follows: (1) Many of its members, but not all, lacked the critical spirit, with the result that they did not weigh evidence severely. In fact, they were inclined to accept as true whatever had got accepted by historians who had already written. (2) Most of the writers in the school, especially those who had the widest vogue, were accustomed to ignore the parts of history that did not seem brilliant. They sought the striking, not only in their choice of subjects, but also in their selection of incident to be made into their narratives. In this process they ignored things relating to every-day life as too common to dignify their stories, and avoided the history of institutions because they considered it dry. (3) It was the custom of these writers to make up their accounts of events by skilfully combining what other writers had said about the same subject. Some of them made little use of original sources which the new school rightly considered the very essence of good history. (4) They did not always restrain their personal feelings in the matters under investigation, with the result that their narratives were apt to defend some particular idea or to attack some other. They had not discovered the sanctity of detachment. (5) Out of the foregoing facts it came about that much that was done by the old school was superficial even where the author had worked with conscientious industry according to the standards before him. Practically the whole body of history prepared by the old school has had to be rewritten by their successors.

It was characteristic of the historians of the old school that they were treated with marked respect by the general public. The men of the first class, nationally known, were received wherever they went as men of national distinction. Those of the second class had relatively similar respect in the smaller areas in which they labored. And this recognition was given as much to history as to the men who wrote it. The age still looked upon Clio as one of the Immortal Nine.

Of all our historians, the one who profited most by this recognition was, perhaps, George Bancroft, who is written down in the early minutes of the American Historical Association as "the father of American History" (*Papers*, 11, 6). Rising into fame through his *History of the United States*, he entered politics and was once a member of the President's cabinet and twice a minister to a foreign country. Setting up his household in Washington in his later life, he became a social lion. He was visited, invited, praised, and honored by the highest people in the land. There was no senator nor cabinet officer who was not pleased to receive his dinner invitations, and his New Year receptions were attended by callers in shoals. He was as popular in his day as a successful play-writer would be to-day. All this superstructure of success was built up, no doubt, by the careful use of specific talents; but it rested fundamentally on his fame as a historian. There was no congressman in the capital who did not know of him as "Bancroft the Historian," and by special action he was given entry at will to the floors of each house of Congress.

Most of these historians were men of independent means: some of them were rich. They had the training and opportunities which usually go with wealth, and in them were developed the standards of taste that commonly come with more than one generation of leisure. Most of them had libraries of their own and counted them adequate for writing history, so that they knew little about the dispiriting desks of public libraries or official-document rooms. Bancroft and Parkman had copies made from archives and even from books in libraries, and Prescott ordered books and transcripts from Europe with a liberal purse.

It is also true that writing history was then financially profitable, as we may see in the following cases: For the *Conquest of Peru* Prescott received $7,500 in cash the day the book went on sale, the edition being 7,500 copies, and for an English edition issued at the same time he got £800. Many later editions were issued, and the total returns were large. Some of Washington Irving's books were accepted by the public as history. For his *Columbus*, his *Voyages of Columbus*, the *Alhambra*, the *Granada*, the *Bonneville*, and *Astoria* he received for the American edition $41,875, and for the

English editions $24,500. Of Motley's *Rise of the Dutch Republic* 15,000 copies were sold in the first year. Bancroft realized a fair fortune from the sale of his history, although a wealthy marriage was the basis of the free expenditure which his high state involved in his later life. When Jared Sparks returned to Boston from Mount Vernon with Washington's papers, to be used in his *Writings of Washington*, he was greeted by Anna Storrow in these words: "I hear you are the richest, the busiest, and the happiest man in New England, perhaps in the world. Long may all this continue!" Returns like these are, perhaps, beyond the day-dreams of the present historian.

The New School

While the old school was at its highest point in the United States, there came into the country the first signs of a movement that was destined to lay it low. It rested on a fundamental kinship to the revolution in natural science then subduing the world. It was critical, impersonal, committed to the study of details, and bent on revising every field of history then written. It expressed its aspirations in declaring that it had "the scientific spirit," which, indeed, was no exaggeration. In its earnestness for truth, it put aside as unimportant the form in which history was written. It did not think of what this meant for the standing of history as a branch of literature. It was too busy with research to think about forms of expression. To its votaries nothing seemed worth considering as an end except the one thing in mind, the realization of truth. Aside from its influence on historical style and its influence on the position of history in the mind of the people, this turning of the historians to the tenets of the new school was the most important thing that has happened in the writing of history in modern times.

The school was rooted in the general revival of ideas in Germany associated with the work of Wolf and the Brothers Grimm; but it was Leopold von Ranke who gave it definite form. His position at the University of Berlin from 1825 to 1871 gave him a wonderful opportunity to shape history in Germany, where so many things were then new. This end was accomplished through a notable group of pupils, who in turn became teachers, among them Waitz, Giesebrecht, and Von Sybel, and also through the series of stately volumes in which his ideas

were exemplified. Of his writing Gooch says:
"Ranke was beyond comparison the greatest
historical writer of modern times." He was
also notable for having established the first
historical seminary. He gathered a group of his
best students around him at Berlin, each working on his own problem, meeting at stated
times. This form of instruction has become the
foundation of advanced teaching in history
from that time to this. It is the keystone of the
new school.

It was not until Ranke's influence ripened
through the success of his many activities that
it began to spread in a notable way to other
countries. In France and England the old
school was well established and doing work
acceptable to the age. But in 1868 Victor Duruy, wishing to introduce the seminary method
of instruction, induced the government to set
up the École Pratique des Hautes Études.
Among the instructors gathered by this school
was Gabriel Monod, a great teacher, a noted
editor, and the founder of the *Revue Historique*,
which became the organ of the new history in
France. The Ranke influence was carried to
England by students, notably by J. R. Seeley,
who became regius professor at Cambridge in

1869. Stubbs took a similar place in Oxford in 1874, and he was thoroughly imbued with the new spirit. In 1873 Oxford set up the honors school of modern history and Cambridge followed suit in 1875 with her history tripos. Ranke's influence was even more marked in Italy, then awakening to a new era of national aspiration, even as Germany had awakened fifty years earlier. It is not possible to dispute the vigor of a system of ideas that had such wide and deep progress in the nations of Europe.

The new school came to the United States by means of returning students who had gone to Germany for instruction. Among them was Charles Kendall Adams, who instituted at the University of Michigan the first historical seminary this country saw. Another was Herbert B. Adams, a student of Wilhelm Ihne's at Heidelberg, who conducted the department of history at Johns Hopkins. Herbert B. Adams took a leading part in collecting the historians of the country into the American Historical Association in 1884. He was made secretary of the organization and gave it freely of his time until the day of his death. The movement spread rapidly. It was a day of reorganization and rapid expansion in our highest education, and the new school easily took possession of the field.

The American Historical Association was in sympathy with the new school. It manifested this fact by electing Ranke its first honorary member, describing him in its minutes as "the oldest and most distinguished exponent of historical science." In accepting election Ranke wrote: "It gives me great satisfaction to belong to a society pursuing beyond the ocean the same aims that we on this side are striving to achieve." While the impulse creating the association came from the young men, the membership included most of the old school, and cordial relations existed between the two wings.

The new type of history had to fight for existence. "Dull and formless scholarship," growled the reviewers, having in mind the clear and charming pages of Prescott. But the young enthusiasts did not falter. They were the new men and the old men died off, so that the new school speedily possessed the field. The critics died off, also, or at least they ceased to carp about style. Perhaps they thought carping useless. Undoubtedly it was wasted effort.

Ranke summed up his purpose in writing history by saying that he tried to tell a thing *wie es eigentlich gewesen,* as it actually happened. That spirit characterizes the entire school that has sprung up under his influence. He never claimed that history was an exact science, but he agreed that it could be written in the scientific spirit. He was pronounced "colorless," and it is true that he did not yield himself to "tides of emotion and outbursts of passion." Restraint and cold white light suited him better. It was the despair of Carlyle, who loved a fine emotion and a towering passion, and he seized on Ranke for the prototype of his "Professor Dryasdust." To which Ranke paid not the slightest attention. He continued to write history *wie es eigentlich gewesen.*

The Attitude toward Style

Ranke's motto implies informational history, and such history became the ideal, consciously or unconsciously, of the school that he founded. It was naturally so, for in trying to tell a thing as it actually happened one is trying to impart information. The writers were deeply absorbed in finding the truth and presenting it as it unfolded in their own minds.

They lost sight of the equally important problem of how to offer information to the minds of their readers. They read a great deal and took notes. Often when they sat down to write they copied note after note into a slightly digested text. Now and again they found that some author had taken a doubtful position, and they introduced into the text a full discussion, with *pros* and *cons*, in their efforts to settle this doubtful point, thereby showing what critical minds they had. These earnest searchers for truth sometimes showed a strong indifference to the rules of rhetoric, they were even careless about grammar. One needs only turn to the doctors' theses of recent years to find many illustrations of these habits. We might be quite impatient of such things, were it not that they have come through an intense search for truth, a thing so valuable in itself that we might pardon any reasonable sacrifice made in its search. But we may well ask, before condemning ourselves to perpetual darkness, if it is necessary for history to become dull in order that it may be written in the scientific spirit.

Professor Robinson seems inclined to answer the question in the affirmative (*New History*, page 51), for he says in this connection: "The

conscientious historian has come to realize
that he cannot aspire to be a good story-teller
for the simple reason that, if he tells no more
than he has good reasons for believing to be
true, his tale is usually very fragmentary and
vague. Fiction and drama are perfectly free to
conceive and adjust detail so as to meet the demands of art, but the historian should always
be conscious of the rigid limitations placed
upon him. If he confines himself to an honest
and critical statement of a series of events as
described in his sources, it is usually too defi-
cient in vivid authentic detail to make a satisfactory story."

Now it is interesting to observe that Professor Robinson himself has written books of
history scientifically admirable, which at the
same time are clear, striking, and interesting
narrative. His text-books in European history
could not have had their wide success if they
had been, to use his own words, "fragmentary
and vague." They are not vague because they
deal with the known facts of the field. Had he
been writing with a great deal more detail he
might have found it necessary to be vague.
But he confined himself to that part of his
field that was known.

Herein lies an explanation of much of the dulness of some of our history. The writer is groping in some field on which the information is limited, and he undertakes to debate the doubtful points before his reader, who has not acquired enough interest in the subject to pay attention to the debate. Such debates used to go into foot-notes, but they are more and more tending to appear in the text. They are highly valuable, but they do not belong in a text that is not intended for the technical reader. "An honest and critical statement of a series of events as described in his sources," says Professor Robinson. The word critical here may be misleading. If the statement embodies the result of criticism, digested in the author's mind and placed in his text as he has adjusted it after mature reflection, it is well. But if it means that the author is to exhibit the critical process to his reader he may not be surprised if the reader is bored. The historian must be critical and the reader should feel that the author is critical; but the average reader does not expect to be called in to see how it is done.

Moreover, it is not just to have history set over against fiction, as though one must write dull arrays of facts or write fiction. The historian does not have to invent in order to tell a clear story. He tells his story, not as the novelist tells one, without limitations, but as one who walks at will within the two walls of fact that keep him in. He does not leap over the walls, but he may walk between them in whatever kind of a line he chooses. His tracks will be rough or symmetrical, as he chooses. He who invents is no historian; he is a falsifier. The new school has lost much good energy in allowing itself to become mystified on this point.

Another point on which it has lost energy by losing hope is by asking itself if history can be literature. The earliest writers in the school, while jumping at the idea that history is a science, were quite willing to say it could not be literature. But as it became evident that history is not a science, they became less confident that it is not literature. At present we are halting at the door, sometimes within it and sometimes without. John Morley defines literature in its most restricted form as "all the books—and they are not so many—where moral truth and human passion are touched with a certain largeness, sanity, and attraction of form." This is a strict standard, but history is not afraid to be measured by it. Always dealing with the moral life of man and with his passions, whether they be expressed in his struggle in the fields of government, economic development, or some less strenuous endeavor, history presents herself to the historian and asks for a treatment that has "a certain largeness, sanity, and attraction of form." Can such a thing be done?

A characteristic commonly accorded to literature, not mentioned in Morley's definition, but implied, perhaps, is imagination. For example, an account of the geological evolution of the earth's surface could possibly be written with the aid of a powerful imagination which would be both science and literature. The imagination is useful to the historian or scientist in enabling him to hold his picture in mind as he paints it. If he writes a lucid and charming piece of prose, it is literature as truly as if he had written a novel or a poem. If Maeterlinck's *Bee* had been written by an entomologist it would have been as truly literature as when written by a dramatist.

A Changing Type

During the last forty years the number of men and women writing history in the United States has largely increased. This result would have occurred through the growth of the country alone and through the spread of education and the development of the educational idea, by which it has come about that a great deal more stress is laid upon history than formerly. It has also been due to a renewed interest in knowing the story of the progress of society here and elsewhere in the world. The type of history that has come to prevail is vigorous and appeals to the man with intellectual taste. The tendency so strongly manifested in the last few years to add to political history the study of social and economic development indicates that we shall have in the future a still larger interest in the subject.

The increased interest in history has produced a stronger call for men to teach and write it. Moreover, the demand came by way of the colleges and universities. Now there were not enough men of the old type interested in history-writing to respond to the demand, and so the deficiency has been made up by calling into service another kind of person.

The old historian was a man of leisure. He had enough means to live on while he got started in the new profession. He could afford to take time to get ready to write. When Prescott decided to become a historian he first mastered modern languages, including English, and then he gave several years to the study of literary expression. Coming across Mably's essay, *Sur l'Étude de l'Histoire*, he read it through ten times in order to absorb its ideas. He made a careful study of the literary structure of Voltaire's *Charles XII* and Roscoe's *Leo X* and *Lorenzo de Medici*. He felt that this kind of preparation was necessary before he took pen in hand. On the composition of his first history, *Ferdinand and Isabella*, he spent ten years.

Prescott could not have subjected himself to this kind of training if he had not had independent means, nor would he have done it if he had not had a well-developed æsthetic sense. To him the painting of an historical picture in words was like an artist's painting of a picture on canvas with pigments. Like the artist, he took time to master the technic of his art.

The æsthetic sense is not a thing that comes hit or miss. One has it by inheritance or by long training in the things that stimulate taste and intellectual harmony. It is more apt to be found in persons who are born of and trained in families of long standing in the upper classes of society than in persons who have sprung from the class that is accustomed to the plainer ways and thinking of the world. The leading historians of the past, for the most part, belonged to this class.

The men going into history to-day do not come from the same social class. An undergraduate body at one of our large universities will contain many students of striking personality, the inheritors of culture by family and class tradition. But of that class almost none go into the graduate schools in the arts. They pass freely into the professional schools of law, medicine, and engineering, but they eschew the non-scientific courses leading to the doctor's degree. Those who offer for the latter courses, and they are numerous, come from another stratum of society. They are usually graduates of the small colleges, the holders of fellowships and to a considerable extent self-supporting while they are students. It is out of such young persons that we are recruiting our college and

university teachers who are to be trainers of
culture for the future.

It would be untrue and also unkind to say
that these persons do not make good teachers
of their subjects. As a class they are as satisfactory in imparting information and in doing the
pedagogical tasks intrusted to them as any
teachers we have ever had. They have good
minds and strong determination. Some of them
show, despite their early lack of taste, remark-
able grasp of its quality. But the majority take
a long time to acquire it, and some never man-
age to reach it. So much the more is it necessary to take some thought of forming their
taste in their early training, so that they will
create an atmosphere of culture in their lec-
ture-rooms and in their writings. Left alone
they are apt to fall into the dull and dreary
habits of amassing information without grace
of form and without charm of expression.

At this point I wish to repeat my caution
that I am not criticising these men as research
scholars. In that respect we have to-day a better situation than we have ever had in the
past. The democratic way of selecting our
teachers and writers by the process of natural
selection has given us sound and industrious

scholarship. The youth of the day are being admirably trained in colleges and graduate seminaries. If to this kind of training we add training in the art of saying things well, we shall have in an approximate way the best results of a democracy.

Probably we need, also, a little more of the spirit of scholarly independence. The spirit of history with us is closely tied up with the desire for an academic career. The young instructor looks to the master who trained him for the help that will lead to promotion in academic rank. Sometimes he goes so far in this respect that he is not willing to give his own spirit full rein to go where he is led by his own thought. Of course, he is not openly conscious of his timidity; but it is at the bottom of his attitude toward his task. If he follows it until the freshness of youth is gone, he becomes a hopeless conservative. It is in the daring of a free mind that we find new life. Nor is it desirable that every man live in fear of the critics. The appearance of a new school of thought is no calamity. Let it battle as it chooses against the old school. Out of the contest will emerge a result which will stand the test of truth.

In this respect we must proceed with caution. Too much daring is a possibility. The youth who ventures into a new view without duly considering his grounds may make a mistake from which many years' labor will not more than free him. It is a calamity for such a man to acquire at the beginning of his career the reputation of being a headstrong fool. Counsel leading to that result is bad. But between the extremes of a too great caution and a rash aggressiveness is a proper middle ground, and he who is wise by instinct can be made to find it. It is out of the men who are wise by instinct that we shall have our good historians.

Another respect in which the personnel of the historians as a class has changed is found in the way in which history-writing in our day has passed into the hands of the teachers of history. The process is as old as Ranke, who was as eminent a teacher as writer. In the old school the historian was rarely a teacher, except as he taught in his books. Moreover, the profession, once it was acquired, was sufficient to give him standing among his fellows, and it yielded him a considerable sum of money. He was willing to risk himself upon it.

This union of history-writing and history-teaching has had some good results. Chiefly it has given the research scholar a standing place. It is hard to see where he would have obtained the means of sustenance while carrying on his research, if he had not a college or university position to rely upon as a means of support. Research in itself does not command enough popular interest to yield that essential return to its devotees. Moreover, the publication of books embodying the results of research gives the scholar additional impetus to conduct his studies, and it is not likely that so many of these works would have been carried to completion if professors had not been engaged in preparing them. Another favorable phase of the matter is that the formulation of a professor's ideas as worked out in his investigations tends to quicken his interest in teaching; and this assertion applies particularly to the young professors. Finally, we have had some professor historians who have achieved excellent results in each field, notably Guizot and S. R. Gardiner, to say nothing of Americans now living. For all these advantages history owes a debt of gratitude to teaching and to the colleges and universities that have made it possible for research to go on.

On the other hand, there are some disadvantages for history in giving her this close dependence on the good-will of another and, to some extent, a different kind of intellectual work. They are so strong that it is worth our while to recount them here and to give the historical student the opportunity to weigh them as they bear on his own personal problems. They may be summed up in the following way:

1. The professor-historian must divide time between two purposes, and since teaching pays his salary it has the preference, not only in his own mind but in the minds of his employers and most of his associates. It follows that he has to write when he finds the time for it, and live where there is employment, regardless of his accessibility to the materials he needs for writing his books. Frequently he is placed where there is little intellectual stimulus and among colleagues who do not appreciate his researches. Or he may fall upon a place where the surroundings, physical or personal, are so charming that he is enticed into wasting time in the mere pleasure of living. This latter peril, often overlooked, has been the undoing of many a man who entered the struggle of his career with a firm determination to produce

books. If he overcomes it, he does it by manly resolve and self-isolation. These difficulties are greater in the United States than in most European countries, because of the greater distances our students must travel to have access to good libraries. In England, for example, one is always in possible reach of the British Museum, wherever he teaches.

2. He has to divide his interest. No man can serve two masters. In the Bible it says that he will love one and hate the other. With respect to the historian who is also a teacher, it is not always true that he will hate one and love the other; it often happens that he comes to love neither. It is necessary that one love in a supreme way the thing he is doing, if he is to do it in such a manner as to lead to the best results. The professor-historian, through taking up one thing and putting down another, may get supremely lost. Sometimes we meet a man who says that he likes teaching and writing equally well, and that he does not know how he could get along without either. Such a man is rarely encountered, and when met he is rarely doing his best in either line.

3. The duties of the pedagogue and the duties of the historian are quite unlike, and the

mind trained in the one may not be most adapted for the other. On one hand, there is the obligation to train and go over the elements of a subject. It is necessary to see that the students who go to college for the "activities" do the minimum of honest labor that is set as a faculty ultimatum. If the professor is dealing with advanced students he must guide their investigations, hear their discussion, and read their theses. This is important work; it may be even more important than writing good history. But it draws out mental faculties unlike those demanded in writing the history that the people wish to read.

4. Finally, history has rights of her own. She deserves and demands a house of her own. Her former state was to be held as one of the highest of the nine muses. The world to-day is bigger and more complex than when she was accorded such dignity. To do her duty by it demands more sacrifice, more ability, and greater service than in olden times. If she does what is expected of her she is a better Clio than ever existed before. It is not treating her with proper courtesy when we tell her she must share lodgings with the pedagogue. It is true that the pedagogue has come up in the world.

He is no longer a slave. He is more worthy of Clio's companionship and he has benefited by the association. But Clio would be more highly respected if she set up her own establishment again.

Of course, it is not very kind to the pedagogues to ask them to give up history-writing, which would well-nigh have disappeared during the last thirty years if they had not kept it alive. In fact, the professors want to write history, and there is no way of keeping them from it as long as they want it. They will go on writing it for many years. But it is possible that, with the growth in this country of a leisure class, or at least of a class of men no longer slaving to make themselves richer, we may find a few men of comfortable means who are willing to devote themselves solely to history. For such men the world will have honor that dollars could not buy and posterity will have blessing, quite as great as if they had endowed benevolent institutions.

Another development of the existing school is the dependence on notes taken as one reads. The old historian depended to some extent on his memory, which is a bad system for any man with a memory less brilliant than Macaulay's.

To supply memory's deficiency we take notes. We take them whenever we come across something of interest. We give them subject titles and file them alphabetically. When we sit down to write we take them out and use them, if we can find them. Now there is a danger in this process, and it has doubtless been a contributing cause of some of the dull history that has been written. A fact remembered is partly assimilated in the mind. A fact tucked away in a collection of notes and forgotten is not assimilated, and when it is brought out for use the writer may be so much engaged on his task of putting together that he does not assimilate. Good books are written in the mind before they are ever put down on paper. The point is that the student should be careful. He need not discard note-taking, but before writing he should spend ample time reflecting upon his notes, throwing out those that are not germane, and getting into the proper perspective those he decides to use. No mechanical contrivance he may have will take the place of a rich, sane, and patient mind.

The Opinions of Two Editors

This discussion of the existing situation will be brought to a close with the opinions of two editors, requested by the writer and furnished by the editors through their sympathy with the purposes of the committee. They come from Doctor John Franklin Jameson, managing editor of *The American Historical Review*, and Mr. Ellery Sedgwick, editor of *The Atlantic Monthly*. Any observations these gentlemen make on the writing of history will be gladly read by students and others interested in history. Whether one agrees with them or not, he will derive much benefit from seeing how the problem appears to them.

Doctor Jameson writes as follows:

"You ask me how the problem of your committee, the problem of considering what could be done to improve the writing of history in this country, looks from the point of view of the editor of *The American Historical Review*. I must say, at once, that I think there can be few points of observation from which that problem can look more urgent or more deserving of thought. Such an editor naturally sees rather more than most others see of the year's product of printed historical work, and certainly he sees an exceptional amount of historical writing in manuscript, offered for publication in his journal. It is distressing to see how little of it is attractively written. Of the printed matter, others have the same opportunity to judge. It is more distinctly in the editor's province to speak of that which comes to his desk in manuscript, and most germane to the present purpose to speak of that which comes from the younger writers, because they are the ones, rather than their more hardened elder brethren, on whose minds the exhortations and suggestions of your committee may be expected to produce some real effect.

"The manuscripts that come to me are not marred by errors of grammar nor by the grosser faults of composition. Minor defects, it is true, abound. Sentences begin with 'However' and 'To be sure' and 'Coincidentally' and 'Due to,' just as they do in the newspapers. Adjectives are used without precision— 'tremendous' often does duty for all adjectives of magnitude. 'Data' in this Latinless age is regarded by some as singular. As to smoothness of expression and consequent ease of reading, it often seems impossible that the writer can have read a single paragraph aloud, else he would have perceived that he was driving over corduroy and not concrete. But the larger and more general fault is a great want of attractiveness. You will not think me to be pleading for flowery rhetoric, and if you remember some of the articles I have printed, you will not suspect me of maintaining too exacting and lofty a standard of style in the case of those I do not print. The plain truth is that, by quite ordinary standards, many of our historical investigators and writers are sadly lacking in the sense of form. Your committee is quite right in inquiring earnestly why this is so, and what can be done about it. It is possible to maintain (it has been done) that history has no business to be either interesting or attractive; but it is not possible to maintain that austere position and at the same time complain that what we write has no effect upon the public mind. And on the whole we all wish that historical writing should be influential.

"What is the reason for these deficiencies? Mainly, I think, that many of those who undertake the writing of history enter upon it with too little of general or literary cultivation, and this is largely because of the habit of specializing prematurely. The more restricted college curriculum of former days did not lay this temptation before the student. I bless Heaven that when as a freshman I resolved to devote the remainder of my years to history, the utmost the college offered in the way of courses in history was one course during one year. I had to spend my college years on a dozen other studies. There was time enough for history afterward. Nowadays I see young men trying to make themselves good historians by 'taking' nothing but history and reading nothing but history, and the university programme, with its ambitiously exaggerated multiplication of courses, aids them in the attempt to do so; but it cannot be done that way.

"There is, moreover, a definite tendency on the part of young men, especially in co-educational institutions, to avoid literary and cultural courses as being feminine. Such courses, they think, are for girls. Though the masterpieces of literature and art and music have mostly been made by men, the American young man has somehow persuaded himself that all this realm is *Frauensache*. It would be agreeable to know more about the best that has been thought and said in the world, but if to follow a literary course will make us seem 'sissified,' it is better to avoid it; there is History 243 that we have not yet 'taken.' The result is to be traced in the plain fact that the young women write much better than the young men.

"Another observable fact, which points in the same direction, is that on the whole the students of European history, young or old, write better than the students of American history. It is, by the way, a great pity that we can so rigidly classify our workers into these two varieties. As a rule, they are completely the one or completely the other. They make their choice early, and for the rest of their lives the student of European history knows very little of American history, the student of American history very, very little of European. I do not know whether there is any greater evil than this in our system of training historical workers. Now the student of European history can hardly escape some contact with European literature and culture, and it will have its effects, however rigidly he may try to confine himself to his *Fach*. The student who has dedicated himself early to American history has perhaps done so because he has a

narrow, a purely national outlook, or because
at his institution the materials for working in
American history seem abundant, those for
European history insufficient, and he is too
poor to go to Europe; or perhaps because
he has not acquired, and shrinks from the
trouble of acquiring, that command of other
languages which is obviously requisite for the
study of European history, but which he
(wrongly) thinks is not needed in purely
American historical studies. But these purely
American studies, however ardently pursued,
will not of themselves do much to improve
his literary taste. Out of 216 American subjects in the last published *List of Doctoral Dissertations in History now in Progress*, I can
count only 25 whose study would lead the
young investigator into the paths of American
or other literature; and of the American historians whom he would be reading, few would
serve him as models of style.

"As for the remedies, while it is perfectly
true that the time for cultivating the sense of
literary form is in the undergraduate period, or
earlier, I recognize that it is not very helpful
to say so. The student's resolve to make history his life-work is ordinarily not taken much

before the end of his undergraduate period. Our real problem lies in the question, what can be done at that late hour to cause him to pay more attention to the quality of his writing. With the need of improvement well impressed upon his mind, and with some free time to devote to it, he is sure to improve. The most direct mode of helping him will be to cause him to read largely in well-written histories, to read continuously and with his mind on the mode of presentation, not, as too often now, to use the great historians merely for looking up points, to make notes, and then to dump his notes undigested into a thesis. But I do not think the professor of history in charge of graduate students should limit his efforts to the promotion of historical reading alone. He should try to lead them into wider fields of literature, should persuade them to repair their deficiencies in cultural subjects, to multiply their contacts with the world of letters, or to increase and enrich whatever humanistic knowledge they may have already acquired. It is easy to say that, if a young man's brain does not naturally generate interesting thoughts, you cannot pump the power into him; but who of us has not risen from the reading of some notable work of lit-

erary art—*Sohrab and Rustum* or *Anna Kare-
nina* or *Java Head*—with the feeling that, for
the time being, at least, he was capable of
richer thought than was within his power before those stimulating contacts?

"It will be asked—it is always asked upon
any suggestion of educational improvement—
how the time for all this is to be found. I answer without hesitation, by shortening greatly
the time required to be spent on the doctoral
dissertation. The amount of time now devoted
to that lucubration—more than a year in many
cases—runs beyond all reasonable limits; in
Serjeant Dunning's phrase, it 'has increased,
is increasing, and ought to be diminished.' The
competitive ambition of graduate schools may
be gratified by the consciousness of producing
the world's biggest theses, but as to the real
good of the student, these swollen volumes of
400, 500, or 600 pages, and the amount of labor expended upon them, are out of all proportion to the benefits. In practical operation a
doctor's degree in history is a certificate that
the young man or young woman is about fit to
begin teaching history in a college. The young
man would in most cases be far better fitted
for that work if, after varied minor researches

in a seminar, he should get the indispensable practice in more extended investigation by preparing a dissertation half as long as is now common (and half as expensive to print), but on a subject so chosen that he would derive from it more varied training, through the use of a wider variety of sources, and if he would use the time thus saved to read—to read histories or whatever else—and to give thought to the ways and forms of presentation, whether in the class-room or in writing."

Mr. Sedgwick's letter is the free statement of a man who has given the subject much thought, and it is thrown off in the interval of a busy editor's life. It presents ideas in a personal and direct way; and for this reason it will be especially valuable to those who are accustomed to theorize. His ideas of the kind of history that would find favor with the reading public will be of service to the historian who asks himself: "What kind of history should I endeavor to write?" The letter is as follows:

"I am only too glad to give you my personal views on the interesting subject of your letter of November 13th. They are of their nature desultory, and simply reflect the experience of an individual who has for a good many years been in touch with a considerable audience of educated people.

"Interest in history has undergone a long and slow decline. The reason is not inherent, for there has certainly never been a time when the lessons of history called for so wide an application. It is the historians themselves who seem at fault. They have catalogued and dissected and subdivided history after the Linnæan plan, dear to the scientific heart, but repugnant to normal human interest. Great historical enterprises, such as the *Cambridge History*, are written by a small and read by a large group of specialists. When they come into the hands of the general public, it is usually through the efforts of the persistent publisher. The ordinary man feels the terrifying complexities of the subject, and knows that to master it in any degree he must wade through a whole series of volumes. He craves two things—a general synthesis whereby he may try at least to see history steadily and whole, and the return of that old-fashioned preoccupation with the leaders of the race, which used to stimulate the imagination and give the personal note which most of us still desire.

"Whatever the learned historian may say, a book like Wells's *Outline* has been a very great stimulus to the study of history. Any man of information can see the bias of the argument and uncounted instances of emphasis wrongly placed, but Wells at least gives him the *habit of perspective*. On the other hand, Wells does not give him those individual, imaginative portraits which once drew the world to Macaulay and Carlyle.

"I believe, therefore, that we need, first, more general histories in which the current of the narrative flows continuously through some considerable period, and, second, biographies *in scale*. Two volumes on President Cleveland or three on Mr. Gladstone represent to the ordinary man mere mismeasurement. Indeed, I wish as a publisher that I might undertake a considerable group of biographies of not more than 40,000 words, somewhat in the character of sustained essays on the significance of individuals. For such a series I should predict marked popularity and usefulness.

"You make special inquiry regarding the attitude of an intelligently conducted magazine toward history. Speaking for *The Atlantic*, I may say that I incline instinctively toward the

publication of original and racy documents—
the story of a Quaker in the Revolutionary
War, the record of an early journey across the
plains, anything of a private and conspicuous
sort which might suggest from its character the
realities of other times. I am also always inclined toward unpublished material dealing
with episodes of importance. Perhaps the best
stroke of this kind that I have been able to
accomplish was the *Diary of Gideon Welles*, of
which a great deal first appeared in *The Atlantic*.

"Finally, there are certain lives in history
which have a magnetism peculiar to themselves. You simply cannot exhaust our public
with Lincolniana, provided the material is
genuine. Garrulous stories from nonagenarians
who have heard Mr. Lincoln speak at Cooper
Union are not wanted, but the smallest attested
facts, if they are characteristic of him, will be
widely read and quoted.

"Perhaps I should amplify what I said about
original history by laying special stress upon
the desirability of publishing important ex-
tracts from diaries. There is nothing like a personal journal for giving a reader at once a sense
of the individuality of the writer and a convic-

tion that the views he expresses are absolutely unvarnished. It is like overhearing an unguarded conversation, and comes home naturally to a man's interest.

"I should like to add a word concerning the great importance of the projected *Dictionary of American Biography*. Valuable from every point of view, it will, if the conduct of the enterprise compares with that of its great British prototype, have an influence which cannot be measured upon the historic preoccupations of our people."

INDEX

Acton, Lord, cited, 19, 73; on the lessons of history, 30.

Adams, Charles Kendall, 107.

Adams, Herbert B., influence on history, 107.

American Historical Association, organized, 93, 98, 102, 107, 108.

American Historical Review, 127.

American histories, 26.

Arnold, Matthew, on the influence of the French Academy, 85.

Bancroft, George, 99; his position in literature, 102; profits from histories, 104.

Benedictines, the French, work for history, 9.

Bodin, Jean, on history, 8.

Bouquet, Father Martin, on history, 9.

Buckle, Henry Thomas, on historians, 65.

Carlyle, Thomas, on history, 109.

Chaucer, on writing, 18.

Cicero, on historical style, 16.

Cicero, on history writing, 8.

Clément, François, on history, 10.

Coulanges, Fustel de, on German historians, 24; on the value of history, 28.

Creighton, Bishop, on history, 13.

Cuvier, task of historian like Cuvier's, 20.

Daunou, Pierre Claude François, on history, 14; on the value of history, 31.

Doctoral theses, 134.

Documents, use of, 19.

Duruy, Victor, influence in France, 106.

Fénelon, on history, 13, 16; on historical detachment, 22.

Flint, Robert, 61.

Fowler, J. H., on writing English, 17.

France, formation of style in, 15.

Gardiner, S. R., profits from his history, 38, 121.

Gibbons, Edward, 55, 58; Macintosh on, 66.

Gooch, G. P., on history, 10.

Graduate instruction and history, 40–54.

Gregory of Tours, 70.

Guizot, François Pierre Guillaume, 121.

Hanotaux, Gabriel, his *Histoire*, 14.

Hartog, P. J., on writing English, 17.

Herodotus, 61.

Historiography, study of, 50.

History, and science, 3, 12; and art, 3; French discussion of, 14; extensive work in, 11; the young writer of, 18; use of documents in writing, 19; as interpreter of facts, 20; and national feeling, 21; and nationality, 21; its value to society, 28–32; effects of commercialism on, 35; state of in the United States, 36; financial profits from, 37; a dull science, 38; influence of scientific spirit on, 40; the reading of, for training, 42; writing of and teaching, 45; the choice of